CHANGING CO

MW00719316

The International Boundary, United States and Mexico, 1848–1963

Also by Robert M. Utley:

The Lance and the Shield: The Life and Times of Sitting Bull

Billy the Kid: A Short and Violent Life

Cavalier in Buckskin: George Armstrong Custer and the Western Military Frontier

High Noon in Lincoln: Violence on the Western Frontier

The Indian Frontier of the American West, 1846-1890

Frontiersmen in Blue: The Unites States Army and the Indian, 1848-1865

Frontier Regulars: The Unites States Army and the Indian, 1866-1891

The Last Days of the Sioux Nation

American Heritage History of the Indian Wars (with Wilcomb Washburn)

CHANGING COURSE

The International Boundary, United States and Mexico, 1848–1963

ROBERT M. UTLEY

SOUTHWEST PARKS AND MONUMENTS ASSOCIATION

Tucson, Arizona

Library of Congress Cataloging-in-Publication Data

Utley, Robert Marshall, 1929–
    Changing course : the international boundary, United States and
Mexico, 1848–1963 / Robert M. Utley, — 1st ed.
        p.   cm.
    Includes bibliographical references and index.
    ISBN 1–877856–29–0 (softcover)
    1. United States—Boundaries—Mexico.   2 Mexico—Boundaries—
United States.   3 Mexican-American Border Region—History.
4. United States—Foreign relations—Mexico.   5. Mexico—Foreign
relations—United States.   I. Title.
F786.U85   1996
327.73072—dc20   96–14212
                                                          CIP

Special contents of this edition copyright © 1996
by Southwest Parks and Monuments Association
All rights reserved. First edition 1996

Design by MIKE YAZZOLINO

Photographs courtesy of Chamizal National Memorial,
except for photograph of Porfirio Díaz on page 56,
courtesy of Arizona Historical Society/Tucson.
Photo number 913334

Epigraph

In the Chamizal Treaty of 1963, the United States and Mexico achieved a friendly settlement of a longstanding dispute over the location of the international boundary between El Paso, Texas, and Ciudad Juárez, Chihuahua. During nearly seven decades of contention over the Chamizal tract, the issue had assumed a significance out of all proportion to the intrinsic value of the land. The treaty by which the problem was at last resolved was a major landmark in the history of Mexican-American relations.

The Chamizal Treaty climaxed more than a century of eventful relations along an international boundary extending from the Gulf of Mexico to the Pacific Ocean. Much of this history was violent and reflected little credit on either nation or its citizens. As the accord that erased the last major international dispute along a boundary fraught with contention for more than a century, the Chamizal Treaty recalls the entire boundary history.

Located on a portion of the land involved in the controversy, Chamizal National Memorial symbolizes the international boundary established in the Treaty of 1963. It stands as a monument to Mexican-American friendship as well as an illustration of events that, though frequently unpleasant, were nonetheless consequential to the history of both nations. This publication traces the history of those events.

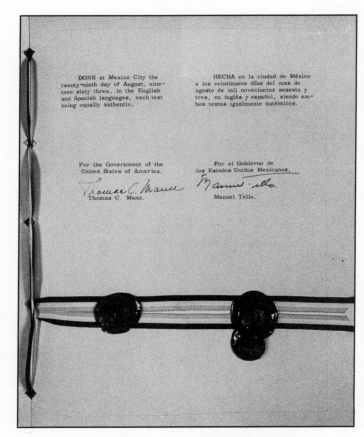

Signature page of the Chamizal Treaty of 1963, which ended 140 years of boundary disputes.

CONTENTS

Good Things Come to Those Who Wait

"Mr. President, the title to the Chamizal Zone has been unsettled for many generations. It is about time that Congress take the necessary steps to resolve the issue."

U.S. SENATOR LYNDON B. JOHNSON

June 9, 1954

On October 28, 1967, thirteen years after Senator Johnson admonished President Dwight Eisenhower that action was long overdue on a thorny diplomatic issue with Mexico, President Lyndon Baines Johnson celebrated in El Paso the fulfillment of his own role in guiding the diplomacy to fruition. In a thinly veiled reference to the history of U.S.-Mexico relations prior to the Chamizal Treaty, Johnson exclaimed, "Too many times has the world seen attempts to change boundaries through force. Let us be thankful that here at Chamizal we celebrate an example of how such matters should be settled."

Not only were there celebrations north of the Rio Grande, but south of the Rio Bravo as well. In 1964, at the close of his six-year term as president of Mexico, Adolfo López Mateos was asked what he considered his most significant accomplishment. "My greatest satisfaction was in having solved the centenary problem of the reincorporation of The Chamizal into the National territory. If Mexico's prestige was increased thereby, its international image strengthened, admiration and respect gained for it in the world, and the independence of its foreign policy secured, my most cherished wishes will have been fulfilled."

Robert Utley is one of the most distinguished and prolific historians on events and themes found in our national parks, monuments, memorials, and battlefields. First written in 1964, the same year López Mateos left office, Mr. Utley's manuscript of *The International Boundary: United States and Mexico* has lingered twice as long to be published as Senator Lyndon Johnson had to wait for the Treaty.

The chronicle of 100 years of bureaucratic and diplomatic foot-dragging leading up to the enthusiastic response from President John F. Kennedy to the 1962 negotiating overture of President López Mateos is absolutely key to a full understanding of the past and current relationships between these two sovereign neighbors. Larger events and more violent episodes loom in the history books to characterize international relations between Mexico and the United States. Despite continuing problems today of trade, commerce, immigration, and environmental quality, one who would understand the tenuous bond between these two old friendly adversaries must also delve into the history and significance of the Chamizal Treaty itself. Recently, for example, it has become better known that President Kennedy's enthusiasm to resolve the Chamizal dispute was at least in part fired by his concern about the Russian military buildup in Cuba. Kennedy did not expect Mexico to be an ally of the U.S. in that showdown, but neither did he want the Mexicans to be unsympathetic to American interests. The motivations for diplomacy are never as simple as they may seem.

Today memorial parks on both sides of the now thoroughly tamed river secure permanent commemoration of the importance of the Treaty and the wisdom of those who crafted it. The U.S. Chamizal National Memorial presents a year round panoply of performing and visual arts to illustrate that people from different histories, traditions, mores, and cultures can learn from and about each other.

The Mexican Chamizal Park includes a pyramid-shaped, polished stone monument erected in honor of the Treaty. Also featured is a modest museum focusing on the archeology, geology, and art of Mexico. Athletic fields and picnic areas are spotted throughout the city park, with emphasis on soccer, one of the national sports.

The entertaining and educational facilities and programs provided in each of these memorial parks are augmented by some of the most appealing and contemplative openspace acres in the region. Both parks have become institutions in this international community, and park managers on both sides of the border have a responsibility to ensure that the noble reasons for which they were established are not forgotten.

Scholars and historians will quibble—as they are supposed to do—about how the history is told, but Utley's account, though researched and written thirty-two years ago, is fresh and illuminating. After all, it was written as events were unfolding that would forever dramatically alter the emotional and geographic connection between the United States and Mexico, the Rio Grande at the Paso del Norte.

BILL SONTAG
Superintendent, Chamizal National Memorial
El Paso, Texas

Establishing the Boundary

1

AT THE DAWN THE NINETEENTH CENTURY, THE YOUTHFUL UNITED States stood on the banks of the Mississippi River and looked across at foreign territory. Less than half a century later, it stood on the shores of the Pacific Ocean. The Louisiana Purchase came from France in 1803 and the Oregon country from Great Britain in 1846, but about half of this enormous territorial expansion was accomplished at the expense of Mexico.

Throwing off the colonial dominion of Spain in 1821, Mexico found itself with a recently defined boundary on the northeast. By the Adams-Onís Treaty, negotiated between the United States and Spain in 1819 but not ratified by Spain until 1822, a line defined roughly by the Sabine, Red, and Arkansas rivers separated Mexico from its neighbor.

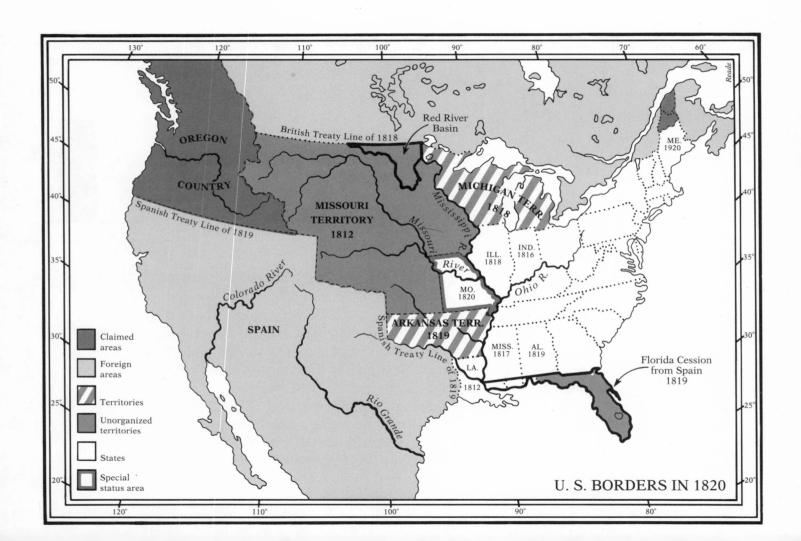

U. S. BORDERS IN 1820

Legend:
- Claimed areas
- Foreign areas
- Territories
- Unorganized territories
- States
- Special status area

OREGON COUNTRY

MISSOURI TERRITORY 1812

SPAIN

British Treaty Line of 1818

Red River Basin

MICHIGAN TERR. 1818

ME. 1920

ILL. 1818

IND. 1816

MO. 1820

Spanish Treaty Line of 1819

ARKANSAS TERR. 1819

Spanish Treaty Line of 1819

LA. 1812

MISS. 1817

AL. 1819

Florida Cession from Spain 1819

Colorado River

Rio Grande

Mississippi R.

Missouri River

Ohio R.

Reade

This boundary meant little to the aggressive Anglo-American frontiersmen swarming over Mexico's northern borderlands—immigrating settlers in Texas, Missouri traders in Santa Fe, fur trappers in the mountains of New Mexico and Sonora, and Yankee sea captains in California. Reeling from repeated political upheavals, the newly independent republic could not withstand the pressures of the expanding northern colossus, whose citizens were adept at discovering biblical injunctions and natural laws commanding them to seize what they coveted.

Texas slipped away in the revolution of 1836 and, to compound the injury, entered the American union in 1845.

Next, in 1846, war broke out. It was set off by a dispute over a narrow belt of uninhabited desert on the southern frontier of Texas, but it afforded the American president, James K. Polk, the opportunity to gain other Mexican possessions deemed important to the national purpose. The guns of the Mexican-American War demolished what was left of the Adams-Onís boundary line. A new one remained to be established.

President James K. Polk.

Opposite: *The United States at the time Mexico won its independence from Spain.*

Treaty of Guadalupe Hidalgo, 1848

As General Winfield Scott's conquering army idled in Mexico City during the closing weeks of 1847, President Polk's peace commissioner wrestled with an agonizing dilemma. His summer's failure to win a treaty from the mercurial Mexican president Santa Anna, together with other actions frowned on in Washington, had led Polk to strip Nicholas P. Trist of his treaty-making powers and order him home. Yet by the time the recall reached Mexico City on November 16, 1847, Santa Anna was no longer in power, and his successors represented a shaky peace party that wanted a treaty at once. They sensed that the country verged on an anarchy that might lead to occupation of all Mexico by the American army and ultimately complete absorption by the acquisitive neighbor to the north. Already, powerful elements in the United States and even among Mexico's propertied classes demanded this very outcome.

Urged on by General Scott, the Mexican authorities, and the resident British and French diplomats, Nicholas Trist gambled. Ignoring the recall, he met with the Mexican negotiators, and on February 2, 1848, they put their signatures to the Treaty of Guadalupe Hidalgo. Although outraged, President Polk feared the political consequences of repudiating the treaty. With the advice and consent of the Senate, he ratified it on March 16, 1848. Ratifications were exchanged with Mexico on May 30, and the treaty was proclaimed on July 4, 1848.

By Nicholas Trist's treaty, an empire passed from one nation to another, an injury to Mexico that the indemnity of fifteen million dollars and relief from the claims of U. S. citizens eased but slightly. Mexico had already lost Texas, annexed by joint resolution of the U. S. Congress in 1845. Now it was forced to recognize the Rio Grande rather than the Nueces River as the Texan boundary and to cede New Mexico and Upper California as well. The latter provinces, long the seat of U. S. commercial interests, had formed President Polk's minimum territorial demand on Mexico. Their acquisition, together with the Oregon settlement in 1846, propelled the western limits of the United States across the Rocky Mountains to the edge of the Pacific Ocean.

Once the extent of territorial cessions had been agreed at Guadalupe Hidalgo, the task of defining the boundaries confronted the treaty negotiators with only slight difficulty. The war had begun in a boundary dispute, and American victory settled that issue. The Rio Grande would divide Texas from Mexico as far upriver as the Chihuahuan city of El Paso del Norte (now Ciudad Juárez).

Trist had tried for both Californias, but the

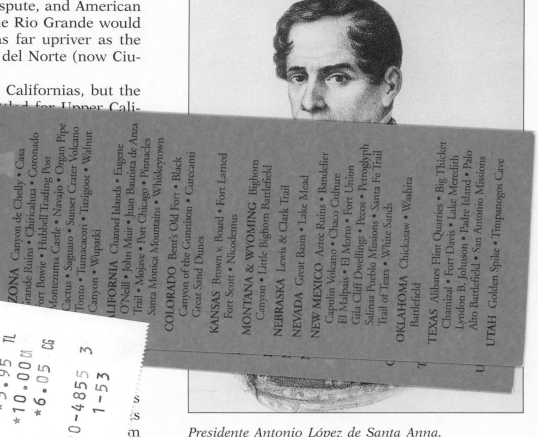

Presidente Antonio López de Santa Anna.

H. Emory had passed down the Gila River in the autumn of 1846. Back in Washington the following summer, he had advised Secretary of State James Buchanan that a railroad could be built down the Gila Valley. The Secretary in turn based his next dispatch to Trist, then with Scott's army in front of Mexico City, on this judgment. In any treaty he might conclude, Buchanan directed, Trist was to try to get the Gila Valley by running the border to its south, along the thirty-second parallel. Instead, Trist settled for the Gila River itself as the boundary.

East from the head of the Gila, the boundary was to follow the line that had divided New Mexico and Chihuahua under Mexican rule to the Rio Grande immediately north of El Paso. Although never surveyed and marked on the ground, this provincial boundary appeared on the 1847 edition of J. Disturnell's "Map of the United Mexican States," a copy of which the diplomats at Guadalupe Hidalgo made a part of the treaty as evidence of where they intended the line to rest in this area.

Trist would have saved both nations much acrimony had he been able to fix the new boundary on the thirty-second parallel as instructed by Secretary Buchanan.

The Joint Boundary Commission

The diplomats had established a boundary. It now remained for the surveyors to accomplish the more daunting task of marking it on the ground. The treaty stipulated that a commissioner and a surveyor representing each nation meet in San Diego within one year after the exchange of ratifications and run the boundary from the Pacific Ocean to the Gulf of Mexico. Their maps and journals defining the boundary were to be regarded as part of the treaty and binding on both countries.

Although the boundary survey got underway at the prescribed time, eight years were to pass before the line was at last laid down on accurate maps and on the earth's surface. These years featured intermittent field work, a diplomatic controversy that drew Mexico and the United States to the brink of another war, and the conclusion of still another major treaty. Throughout, while the two nations hurled threats and imprecations

Opposite: *Annexed to the Treaty of Guadalupe Hidalgo, the Disturnell map became the focus of bitter contro*versy.

at each other, the Mexican and American officials of the Joint Boundary Commission got along famously and set an example of understanding, teamwork, and good humor that served as a reproach to their superiors in Washington and Mexico City.

Among themselves, by contrast, the Americans feuded incessantly. Buffeted by political winds from Washington and consumed with petty quarrels over authority and perquisites, the United States section of the commission rocked with internal dissension for four years until finally given a thorough cleansing. Only then did the survey proceed with efficient dispatch.

Most of the trouble sprang from the mixed character of the American section. The commissioner and surveyor were both politically appointed civilians, as were other lesser functionaries. The army's elite Corps of Topographical Engineers furnished the technicians who were to do much of the field work, and the dragoon and infantry escorts came from the line of the army. The operation was placed first under the State Department and then, late in 1849, under the newly created Department of the Interior. With vague lines of authority and overlapping functions, it was an organization that invited conflict between civilian and military personnel.

Before turning over the presidency to Zachary Taylor early in 1849, Polk appointed Ohioan John B. Weller as U. S. commissioner and Texan Andrew B. Gray as surveyor. Brevet Major William H. Emory, the able topographical engineer who had alerted Secretary Buchanan to the railway possibilities of the Gila Valley, headed the military contingent as "Chief Astronomer and Commander of the Escort."

At San Diego early in July 1849, these men met their Mexican counterparts, General Pedro García Condé, commissioner, and Major José Salazar y Larregui, surveyor. Condé was a former Mexican Secretary of War and Navy, Salazar a distinguished military engineer. Both turned out to be cultured gentlemen and charming companions.

Democrat Weller had no sooner reached California in the early summer of 1849 than the new Whig administration in Washington decided that his post belonged to a loyal Whig. The stormy John C. Frémont, lately dropped from the

Opposite: *The boundary between the U. S. and Mexico as committed to in the Treaty of Guadalupe Hidalgo.*

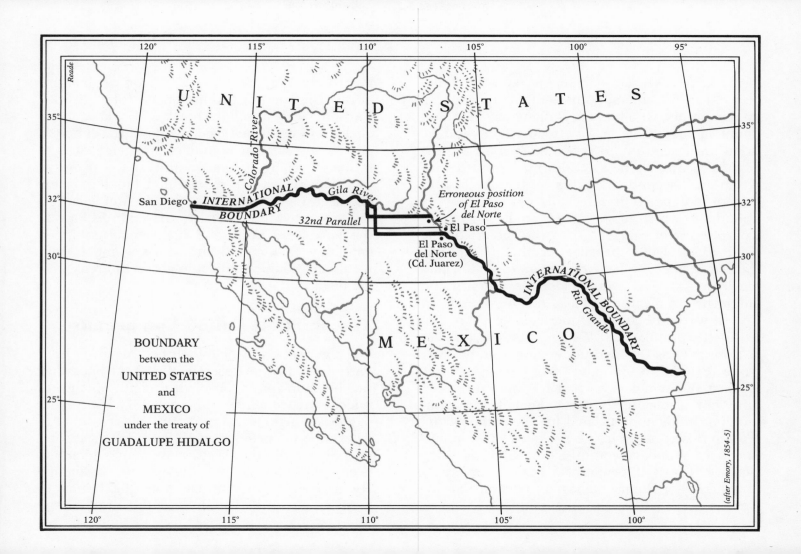

BOUNDARY
between the
UNITED STATES
and
MEXICO
under the treaty of
GUADALUPE HIDALGO

army after a sensational, highly political court-martial, won the appointment. This angered Major Emory, who had been aligned against Frémont in the events leading to the trial, and he tried unsuccessfully to resign from the commission. The travel time to California, coupled with Frémont's second thoughts over whether to accept the position after all, gave Weller six months in which to start the boundary from the coast south of San Diego to the mouth of the Gila River. Here, because of the disruptions caused by the stampede of miners to California's newly discovered gold fields, the commission adjourned to meet in El Paso in November 1850.

It would be, on the American side, a reconstituted commission. Weller was out, off to Washington as Democratic senator from the new state of California and nursing grievances against the Whigs, who had not only displaced him but also ruined him financially by withholding funds appropriated for the commission. Frémont was never in; he pocketed his appointment as boundary commissioner and, as Whig senator from California, also headed for Washington. Major Emory managed to get off the survey as well, although only temporarily as it turned out. Only Gray, the surveyor, retained his post. The new commissioner, John Russell Bartlett, was a scholarly New England book dealer and publisher specializing in travel books. Travel, rather than boundary surveying, was to be his specialty in the Southwest too. Emory's replacement was an elderly and bibulous army engineer, Lieutenant Colonel John McClellan. At the appointed time, Bartlett arrived in El Paso at the head of a large and luxuriously equipped entourage that caused him nearly as much trouble as the boundary dispute about to break over his head.

The Bartlett-Condé Compromise

The commissioners held their first meetings in El Paso del Norte in December 1850. At once they ran head-on into a problem difficult enough to understand, much less to resolve. The surveyors had been making astronomical observations to determine the position of El Paso del Norte, and they discovered that Disturnell's map, which had been annexed to the Treaty of Guadalupe Hidalgo as a guide to defining the boundary between the Rio Grande and the head of the

Gila, contained errors of both latitude and longitude. The map showed El Paso del Norte at latitude 32° 15′, whereas it actually lay thirty-four miles to the south, at latitude 31° 45′. To compound the confusion, Disturnell placed the Rio Grande (and therefore El Paso) at longitude 104° 39′, one hundred miles east of its true position at 106° 29′. By the map's scale, the southern boundary of New Mexico, the prospective international boundary, ran westward from a point on the Rio Grande eight miles north of El Paso.

Two questions confronted the commissioners. Should the initial point of the boundary on the Rio Grande be established according to the map's scale—eight miles north of El Paso—or according to its latitude—forty-two miles north of El Paso? And should the line run three degrees of longitude west of the Rio Grande as it appeared on the map or as it was actually located on the earth? General Condé naturally argued that the boundary must be determined by reference to latitude and longitude as marked out on the map, even though erroneously. Bartlett contended that the map's scale must control, for this was the only evidence the treaty negotiators could possibly have considered.

Compromise was clearly in order, and Bartlett rose to the occasion. In effect, he traded Condé latitude for longitude. The initial point would be fixed on the Rio Grande at 32° 22′, or forty-two miles north of El Paso, and the line would extend westward three degrees, or 175.28 miles, from the river's true longitude.

To make the agreement legal, the commissioner and surveyor of each nation had to sign. Condé, Salazar, and Bartlett signed, but Surveyor Gray, detained by illness in Texas, had not yet arrived. Colonel McClellan had been recalled to save him the embarrassment of facing Bartlett's charges of drunkenness, and his successor, Lieutenant Colonel James D. Graham, was still en route. Bartlett thus pressed Lieutenant Amiel W. Whipple, acting for both Gray and Graham, into service as surveyor *ad interim* to sign the agreement, which he did under protest. On April 24, 1851, in a ceremony sparkling with cordiality, the officials erected the initial monument on the river at 32° 22′, and astronomical parties began running the boundary westward.

Bartlett was well pleased. Condé, he knew, could never have yielded to the American contention, for in the loss of Texas, New Mexico, and

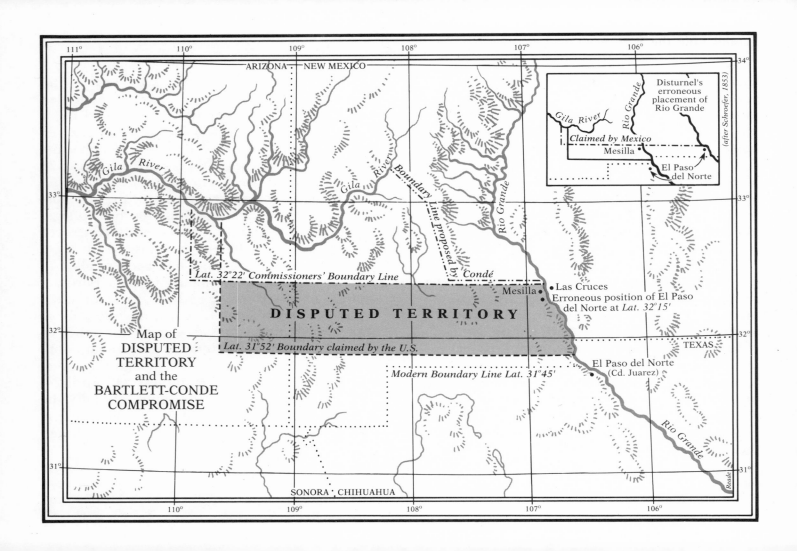

Map of DISPUTED TERRITORY and the BARTLETT-CONDE COMPROMISE

ARIZONA · NEW MEXICO

Gila River

Gila River

Gila River

Boundary Line proposed by Condé

Rio Grande

Lat. 32°22′ Commissioners' Boundary Line

DISPUTED TERRITORY

Mesilla ● ● Las Cruces
● Erroneous position of El Paso
del Norte at *Lat. 32°15′*

Lat. 31°52′ Boundary claimed by the U.S.

TEXAS

Modern Boundary Line Lat. 31°45′

El Paso del Norte
(Cd. Juarez)
●

Rio Grande

SONORA · CHIHUAHUA

Inset:

Disturnel's erroneous placement of Rio Grande

Gila River

Rio Grande

Claimed by Mexico

● Mesilla

● El Paso
del Norte

(after Schroeter, 1853)

Reade

California his countrymen had already suffered a severe blow to their national pride. Moreover, Bartlett believed that the United States had got the better of the bargain. Except for the fertile Mesilla Valley along the Rio Grande between the initial point and El Paso, the United States had given up nothing but a desert and in return had gained mountains that contained the rich Santa Rita copper mines.

But Bartlett minimized one momentous consideration—the Pacific railway, which had taken on new importance with the discovery of gold in California in 1848. In 1851 no one dreamed that more than one transcontinental railroad would ever be built. Such expert opinion as could be found, chiefly of army officers who had glimpsed some shadowy outlines of southwestern geography during the Mexican-American War, supported the South's contention that the best and possibly the only way to span the continent was to run the rails around the southern end of the Rocky Mountains. Conveniently, engineering realities seemed to further the political and economic objectives of the South.

When Surveyor Gray finally reached commission headquarters at the Santa Rita mines in July, he was appalled to find that the railway route so vigorously championed by his home state of Texas had been bargained away by the commissioner from New England. Gray refused to sanction the Bartlett-Condé agreement and contended that it had no force without his signature. When Colonel Graham arrived on the scene, he supported Gray and called in Lieutenant Whipple's surveying parties from the compromise line. Work came to a halt.

The Bartlett-Condé compromise set off a storm of controversy in Washington and elsewhere in the nation. The Whig administration of Millard Fillmore (who had succeeded to the presidency on the death of Zachary Taylor) supported its commissioner, but expansionist Democrats had no intention of surrendering.

In the Southwest, new complications set in. Surveyor Gray and Colonel Graham fell to quarreling over rank and authority. The able General Condé, "an amiable and estimable gentleman," in Bartlett's opinion, took ill and on December 19, 1851, died at his home in Arispe, Sonora. And

Opposite: *The disputed alternative boundaries.*

Bartlett himself, while Gray and Whipple worked the Gila, plunged into northern Mexico ostensibly in search of supplies. For the adventure-loving bookman, it was a grand junket that lasted a full year and carried him deep into Sonora to Mazatlan, by steamer to San Diego, and, after a tour of California, overland to El Paso.*

Meanwhile, the composition of the American team had shifted again. The Secretary of the Interior had removed Gray from the surveyor's post, and the army had recalled Colonel Graham. Major Emory found himself once more on the commission, this time as replacement for both Gray and Graham.

Reaching El Paso in November 1851, as Bartlett lay ill with fever in Ures, Sonora, the new surveyor-astronomer wrote to an eastern friend: "On my arrival here I found things more complicated than I had expected, a large party, half with Colonel Graham at this place, and the

---

*Although Bartlett's journey accomplished nothing for the boundary survey, historians will ever be grateful for the detailed descriptions that he left in his book, *Personal Narrative of Explorations and Incidents in Texas, New Mexico, California, Sonora and Chihuahua . . .*, published in two volumes in New York in 1854.

other half with Mr. Bartlett God-knows-where, the whole numbering one hundred and upwards, no money, no credit, subdivided amongst themselves and the bitterest feeling between the different parties. Little or no work has been done, and yet the appropriation is all gone and that of next year anticipated."

Emory carried peremptory orders from his appointing authority, the Secretary of the Interior, to sign the Bartlett-Condé agreement and thus stamp it with the legality expansionists denied it because of the absence of Gray's signature. The major had no wish to endorse the agreement, however, for he now perceived that the problem involved more than simply obtaining the Disturnell treaty line instead of the Bartlett-Condé line. As early as 1850, while first on the boundary commission, Emory had concluded that, contrary to his judgment of 1847, a sizable tract of country south of the Gila would be required for the railroad. He had unsuccessfully advocated a complicated process that he thought gave some hope of "torturing the Treaty of Guadalupe Hidalgo to embrace a practicable route."

In Emory's opinion, then, neither line would win the United States the corridor it sought. But to authenticate the Bartlett-Condé agreement would settle the issue and close the door to further negotiations. By alienating congressional expansionists, moreover, it might also have an adverse effect on his career. On the other hand, refusal to obey the order to sign could smash his career at once. Emory came up with a solution that protected his career while also leaving expansionists free to continue agitation of the issue. In August 1852 he signed the document as ordered, but with the reservation that it implied no more than witnessing an agreement already reached by the two commissioners.

Harassed by financial troubles, Emory spent most of 1852, in Bartlett's absence, surveying the Rio Grande frontier. The commissioner, arriving in El Paso in August 1852 after his year-long tour of Sonora and California, now decided to take a circuitous route to the rendezvous with Major Emory. A swing south by way of the capital of Chihuahua and a march across Coahuila brought him at last, in December 1852, to Emory's headquarters at Ringgold Barracks (Eagle Pass), Texas. Here Bartlett found Emory with no money and exhausted credit.

Here also Bartlett found himself, by action of the U. S. Congress, out of a job. Expansionist Democrats had saddled the commission's appropriation with an amendment prohibiting any part being spent "until it should be made to appear to the President of the United States that the southern boundary of New Mexico had not been established further north of El Paso than is laid down on the Disturnell Map." The president concluded that the money could not be spent, and he ordered the commissioner to suspend operations. Bartlett retired to Providence, Rhode Island, to write his fascinating travelogue.

Until the congressional intervention, the disputed territory had been in dispute mainly between Whigs and Democrats in the United States, although the issue cut across party lines where party and sectional interests diverged. The Mexican role had been chiefly one of urging her neighbor to get on with carrying out an agreement made in good faith by representatives of both nations. With the repudiation of the Bartlett-Condé compromise, however, the tract between the Disturnell treaty line and the Bartlett-Condé line formed a diplomatic battleground. Paradoxically, it was the narrow band of irrigated farmland in the Mesilla Valley rather than the prospective railway route across the desert to the west that moved the dispute into crisis.

Both Mexicans and Americans lived in the Mesilla Valley. Mexican authorities contended that these settlers wanted Mexican rule, New Mexican officials that they favored and expected American rule. In 1851, after conclusion of the Bartlett-Condé compromise, Chihuahuan officials took over the Mesilla Valley west of the Rio Grande as far as the initial point established by the two commissioners and decreed that American citizens could not hold land in the valley. Respecting the Bartlett-Condé line, Governor James S. Calhoun of New Mexico ignored the anguished protests of the affected Americans.

Congressional repudiation of the compromise line changed the equation. In March 1853 the new governor of New Mexico, William Carr Lane, issued a provocative proclamation asserting authority over the contested tract. Chihuahuan Governor Angel Trias responded in kind and moved soldiers into the Mesilla Valley. Only the uncooperative stance of the military commander in New Mexico, Colonel Edwin V. Sumner, restrained Governor Lane from trying to occupy the valley at once. Then Lane received a letter from the U. S. minister in Mexico City warning of the "extreme gravity" of the situation and suggesting that he "gracefully" moderate his attitude, which he did. David Meriwether soon replaced Lane as governor of New Mexico with instructions to take no action to alter the *status quo* in the Mesilla Valley.

By the middle of 1853, Mexican-American relations had fallen to their lowest ebb since the war. The two nations confonted each other menacingly in the Mesilla Valley. The boundary dispute seemed unsolvable by means other than war. The boundary survey had been suspended far short of completion. And increasing awareness of topographical realities favored Major Emory's contention that the disputed territory alone would not accommodate a railroad to the Pacific.

Other issues fell into the mix. The United States had promised in the Treaty of Guadalupe Hidalgo to prevent resident Indians from raiding in Mexico. It had signally failed and, with Mexican claims mounting, wanted to be free of the obligation. Also, a group of Americans demanded government help in forcing Mexico to make good on previous promises of land grants for a canal and railroad across the Isthmus of Tehuantepec. And finally, the old issue of the claims of American citizens against Mexico had once more intruded on diplomacy. To the incoming Democratic administration of Franklin Pierce, who took office in March 1853, a major diplomatic effort to settle these problems seemed pressing.

The Gadsden Treaty, 1853

As U. S. minister to Mexico, President Pierce appointed James Gadsden, South Carolina railroad executive, champion of the southern rail route to the Pacific, and ardent exponent of a commercial alliance of South and West to check the growing political and economic ascendancy of the North. Gadsden's primary mission was to negotiate a treaty with Mexico that would resolve all outstanding problems.

The most urgent and significant problem was the boundary. Secretary of State William L. Marcy instructed Minister Gadsden to treat for the purchase of the zone south of the Gila River needed for a railway route. While disavowing the legality of the Bartlett-Condé line, he was to merge the discussion of the disputed territory with negotiation for the purchase of additional land. Gadsden was also to reject Mexican claims for depredations committed by American Indians

in Mexico and to gain release from the treaty obligation to prevent such depredations. Finally, he was to negotiate a settlement of all claims by citizens of one nation against the other.

Thus when Gadsden departed for Mexico City in the summer of 1853, his major purpose was to obtain enough land for a railway south of the Gila River. By autumn this objective had grown. In Mexico Gadsden found the regime of President Santa Anna bankrupt and verging on overthrow by revolutionary forces. Only money could stave off collapse, and even then only if swiftly forthcoming. Gadsden informed his superiors that money and not territory would control the negotiations. President Pierce promptly dispatched a special emissary, Christopher Ward, with new instructions authorizing Gadsden to try for much more territory.

There were five options, each based on a natural and easily defended frontier. The most ambitious, for which Gadsden could offer up to $50 million, would annex all Lower California and large parts of Sonora, Chihuahua, and Coahuila. By running the boundary along the almost impassable rampart of the Sierra Madre, this option would supposedly reduce border frictions.

James Gadsden, negotiator of the famous Gadsden Purchase.

The least ambitious, a final resort only after the other four were rejected, offered $15 million for a boundary on the thirty-second parallel. This would give the United States nothing more than the coveted railway route.

Gadsden had overstated Santa Anna's readiness to part with his nation's soil. The staggering territorial loss had made the Mexican people extremely sensitive to any suggestion of further loss, no matter how small or for what compensation. Santa Anna knew that he courted revolt by considering even the minimum American proposal. Nevertheless, such was the compelling need for money, he agreed to negotiate on the basis of the fifth proposal—only sufficient territory for a railroad.

Santa Anna later explained that an empty treasury and impotent army left him no choice but to sell or face another war, which Mexico could only lose. According to the Mexican president, Gadsden had asserted that the railway was vital to the United States and "he would be pleased if Mexico would cede peaceably and for a good indemnity that which possibly did belong to her; for in the end that imperious necessity would compel them to occupy it in one way or another."

Santa Anna's charge that Gadsden presented the issue in terms of sell or be dispossessed is probably correct. Santa Anna sold. The "Treaty of Boundary and Cession of Territory" was signed at the U. S. Legation in Mexico City on December 30, 1853.

Docking at New Orleans early in January 1854, the American envoy declared to the customs officer: "Sir, I am General Gadsden. There is nothing in my trunk but my treaty." Actually, Christopher Ward bore the treaty to Washington, but Gadsden had indeed negotiated an important accord. It gained the southern railway route by describing a new boundary that gave the United States the disputed territory as well as a broad belt of land adjoining it on the west. It secured release from the vexatious commitment to restrain Indian raiders in Mexico. It adjusted the claims question, including the vigorously pressed claims relating to the rail and canal route across the Isthmus of Tehuantepec. And it reaffirmed the expressions of amity contained in the Treaty of Guadalupe Hidalgo. For all these concessions, the United States was to pay Mexico $15 million and assume up to $5 million of the private claims of its citizens against Mexico.

Although highly favorable to American interests, the Gadsden Treaty still had to run the gauntlet of the U. S. Senate, where it arrived in the midst of a passionate debate over the Kansas-Nebraska Bill. This had reopened the sectional wounds that moderates thought had been closed by the Compromise of 1850. Northern senators saw in the Gadsden Treaty one more piece of a southern conspiracy to gain additional territory into which slavery might expand. Other senators opposed it because it did not annex even more territory, particularly enough to gain the United States a port on the Gulf of California. Still others, champions of more northerly transcontinental rail routes, viewed it as raising a serious threat to these routes. And finally, a powerful bloc of senators representing the Tehuantepec grantees would accept no treaty that did not specifically recognize their claims.

The treaty did, but it came to the Senate with the president's recommendation that the recognition be struck out. The revised terms of reference relayed to Gadsden the previous October had said nothing about injecting this matter into the negotiations. To maintain secrecy, however, the new instructions had been memorized by the courier, Christopher Ward, and conveyed orally to Gadsden. Ward, it turned out, was financially interested in the Tehuantepec grant, and to Gadsden he represented the president as desiring the claims recognized in the treaty. Gadsden successfully inserted the recognition.

President Pierce was furious, and only the persuasion of Senator Thomas J. Rusk, the southern railway champion from Texas, induced him to send the document to the Senate at all. Although of no consequence to the national interest, the Tehuantepec issue played a vital, even decisive, role in the ultimate fate of the treaty.

Most of the debate centered on the boundary. Since the extreme antislavery senators planned to vote against the acquisition in any form, the debate was mainly between those content with only a railroad route and those who wanted still more territory. Amendments to augment the cession were voted down, however, and Senator Rusk at last defined a line that, with a slight modification, was accepted: west one hundred miles from an initial point on the Rio Grande at 31° 47', then south to parallel 31° 20', then west on this parallel to its intersection with the 111th meridian, then in a direct line to the Colorado River twenty miles below its confluence with the Gila, then up the Colorado to the established boundary and west on it to the Pacific.

That the amendment reduced the cession as defined in the treaty by nine thousand square miles reveals that most of its promoters were concerned mainly with securing a railway route and were willing to placate the antislavery wing as much as possible consistent with this purpose. The curious southward turn of the line in what is now southwestern New Mexico reflected Senator Rusk's assessment that the territory added thereby was needed for the railroad. Having reduced the territory to be ceded, the senators then also reduced the compensation—from $15 million plus $5 million in private claims to $10 million with no mention of claims.

By striking all reference to private claims, the Senate dropped the specific recognition of the Tehuantepec claimants. Thus when the amended treaty came to a vote on April 17, 1854, after more than a month of bitter debate, it went down to defeat by a count of twenty-seven to eighteen. Champions now inserted provisions favorable to the Tehuantepec grantees and gained the necessary votes. On April 25 the Senate advised and consented to the ratification of the Gadsden Treaty as amended. On June 30, 1854, ratifications were exchanged in Washington, D.C., and the Gadsden Treaty was proclaimed the same day.

A curious epilogue ended the diplomatic phase of the Gadsden Purchase. On June 30, the day the treaty was proclaimed, Mexico received $7 million as a first installment of the payment. The remaining $3 million would be released on completion of the boundary survey. But Santa Anna's corrupt regime went through the $7 million in three months and demanded the additional $3 million at once. When the United States refused, he resurrected the old issue of the Mesilla Valley.

Although the boundary had not been run, no one questioned that the Mesilla Valley lay within the ceded territory. Therefore, to provide a stable government, Governor David Meriwether extended the authority of the Territory of New Mexico over the valley. Federal troops crossed the river, and on November 16, 1854, the U. S.

flag rose ceremoniously over the Mesilla plaza. (Today, because of the shifting course of the river, Mesilla is on the east side of the Rio Grande.)

Mexico protested that the American action fully justified the entire payment. The State Department refused to relent, but suffered through repeated demands until the boundary survey was at last completed in 1856. By then Santa Anna had been overthrown, and the $3 million went to the successor regime.

The Gadsden Purchase rounded out the continental boundaries of the United States and gained a land that eventually proved rich in minerals and agricultural potential. It also won southerners their long-sought railway route. To settle the persistent controversy over the best way across the continent, Congress in 1853 authorized the army's Topographical Engineers to examine all the proposed routes. Lieutenant John G. Parke explored in the Gadsden Purchase in 1854 and again in 1855 and reported that it offered all the advantages claimed by its supporters.

But the Pacific Railway Surveys disclosed that several other routes were also feasible, and anyway the true issues were political and economic, not engineering. The Civil War resolved these issues in favor of the North. In 1862, in the midst of the war, Congress sanctioned the Pacific Railway along a central route. The southern route was not even considered.

Even so, it earned its place in history. The first transcontinental stagecoach service, inaugurated in 1858 by the Butterfield Company, followed Lieutenant Parke's survey across the Gadsden Purchase. Then in 1880 completion of the Southern Pacific Railroad along the Parke line at long last realized the dreams of those prewar expansionists who had insisted on a new boundary for the Southwest.

General Gadsden's treaty had turned out to be a valuable trunkful.

Marking the Boundary

2

THE ACTUAL SURVEY OF THE MEXICAN-AMERICAN BOUNDARY WAS an achievement of great significance to both nations. It fixed on the face of the land, presumably for all time, the international boundary. Of perhaps even greater significance, it filled in the physical and natural outlines of the newly acquired American Southwest. It gave cartographers for the first time accurate and detailed maps of the Southwest. It gave the maturing American scientific community informative texts and professional illustrations illuminating the topography, geology, botany, zoology, and ethnology of the Southwest. In short, it made an unknown country known in all its features. With the Mexican War reconnaissances, the Pacific Railway surveys, the wagon road program, and other official and private explorations of the 1850s, the International Boundary Survey provided the nation with the knowledge it needed to move west knowingly.

The boundary survey, moreover, was an adventure in the best frontier tradition. The surveyors had to make laborious observations and computations under conditions of climate and terrain adverse to man, beast, and the fragile instruments of the profession. They had to penetrate deserts, mountains, and canyons that other travelers could avoid. They had to find water in an often waterless land. They had to supply themselves by wagon or mule from distant bases over great stretches of difficult country. They had to keep always alert for Indians and be prepared at all times to fight them. This and more they did, and their adventures form some of the most dramatic episodes in the history of the American West.

The boundary survey was a monument to many men of both Mexico and the United States—to military and civilian engineers; to the assistants who did their leg work; to geologists, botanists, zoologists, and artists who revealed a strange new world to the people back home; to political spoilsmen who measured up to the task

and to those who did not; and to the officers and soldiers of the military escorts who guarded against Indians and performed a variety of supporting functions.

But most of all the boundary survey was a monument to two skilled and dedicated engineers who first met in 1849 for the survey of the southern boundary of California, who cooperated on the survey of the river frontier, who together ran the Gadsden Purchase line, and who finally parted, the job finished, eight years later. Both often lacked the support of their respective governments, and both often contended with political forces that had no proper place in such an undertaking, but both persevered and ultimately triumphed. Because of Major William Helmsley Emory and Major José Salazar y Larregui, the international boundary was laid down on the map and on the ground.

The Southern Boundary of California, 1849–51

Awarding Upper California to the United States, the Treaty of Guadalupe Hidalgo specified that, "in order to preclude all difficulty of tracing on the ground the limit separating Upper from Lower California, it is agreed that the said limit shall consist of a straight line drawn from the middle of the Rio Gila, where it unites with the Colorado, to a point on the coast of the Pacific Ocean one marine league due south of the southernmost point of the port of San Diego." Marking this 148-mile segment of the new international boundary was the first task the treaty set for the recently appointed commissioners, Bartlett and Condé.

The Joint Boundary Commission organized in San Diego early in July 1849. The United States section numbered 39 men, both civilian and military, and an escort of 105 soldiers. The Mexican engineers were fewer and less elaborately equipped, but boasted an escort of 150 veteran Indian fighters from Sonora. Political and financial harassments immediately beset the commission, as the new Whig administration in Washington withheld funds and set about displacing Commissioner Weller. In addition, the first wave of the California gold rush rolled over the Sierra Nevada in this year. All but a handful of the civilian laborers attached to the survey deserted to the mines, and the bankrupt commission could

Major William Emory, U.S. survey leader for the boundary.

not begin to keep up with the soaring cost of food and other supplies.

The prosecution of the survey in the field fell to the "Chief Astronomer and Commander of the Escort," Major Emory. Maryland aristocrat, West Point graduate, able engineer and accomplished gentleman, Emory personified the best in the emerging professionalism of the United States Army.

Quickly Emory gained effective control of the operation. In him both commissioners recognized a man of superior scientific attainments, and they bowed readily to his advice. Commissioner Weller was absent most of the time trying to raise money, and the other principal civilian member of the American contingent, Surveyor Gray, did not accomplish much. Emory's military status enabled him to employ soldiers in place of the civilian laborers who had vanished into the mining districts and to requisition stores from the army post at San Diego. The Mexicans could contribute little. Although "well-educated and scientific men," in Emory's opinion, they brought instruments that proved entirely unreliable, and they confined themselves, after checking the observations and calculations of the Americans, to certifying the conclusions as correct and acceptable to Mexico.

Aside from the burdens imposed by politics in Washington and conditions in California, the surveyors faced nearly insurmountable topographical obstacles. The boundary fell across a country half mountain and half desert. The mountains rose steeply from the coast to an elevation of five to six thousand feet, then rolled eastward for thirty miles in a succession of parallel ridges cut by deep canyons. Abruptly, then, the desert took over, with shifting sands devoid of vegetation stretching from the eastern flank of the mountains to the Colorado River. (Transformed by irrigation, this desert is now the garden spot of Imperial Valley.)

This country was a surveyor's nightmare. To maintain field parties in such rough, waterless, sun-baked terrain for the time necessary to make the complicated observations and computations of a boundary survey was an assignment that taxed the resources of Americans and Mexicans alike.

The procedure was to determine the precise latitude and longitude of each of the initial points and run an astronomical line between them. In July Emory established Camp Riley south of San Diego, set up his instruments, and began the tedious observation of moon and stars necessary to reach an accurate determination of latitude and longitude.

Lieutenant Amiel W. Whipple, delayed by supply difficulties, left in September to lead a party across to the Colorado and establish the other terminal point. Setting up an observatory atop an eminence he named "Capitol Hill" near the mouth of the Gila River, he too began the nightly labor of recording astronomical readings.

A third party, under Brevet Captain Edmund L. Hardcastle and assisted at times by Surveyor Gray, explored the mountains behind San Diego. Emory hoped to hasten the running of the line by "flashes"—gunpowder explosions—observed at night through surveying instruments, and Hardcastle's mission was to discover if the topography lay in proper arrangement to make this method feasible.

Although the observations at Camp Riley continued from late July well into November, Emory and the Mexican surveyor, Major Salazar, agreed to the location of the initial point on the Pacific in October 1849. The treaty placed it one marine league south of the southern tip of San Diego Bay, but there was no accepted standard for a marine league. After some debate, the officers settled on an arbitrary measurement of 5,564 meters (three and one-seventh miles). The distance was then measured on the ground and the latitude and longitude of the spot determined by trigonometric triangulation from the known position of nearby Camp Riley. The initial point of the boundary was now laid down on the ground and on the map.

At the other end of the line, Lieutenant Whipple grappled with distractions. Contending with swarms of destitute gold seekers piling up at the Yuma Crossing of the Colorado River, he also had to divert manpower for a reconnaissance to locate a suitable place for the army to build a fort. By early November, however, Whipple had completed his calculations, and Major Salazar came over to confirm the findings on behalf of Mexico. Then, by direct measurement from the determined position of the observatory on Capitol Hill, they computed the latitude and longitude of the junction of the Colorado and Gila rivers.

It now remained to connect the two known points by the azimuth of a straight line on the earth's surface and to place boundary monuments along it. Emory's hope that this might be accomplished by the speedy and accurate flash system dissolved as Captain Hardcastle's explorations disclosed unfavorable topography.

In December 1849, moreover, Weller at last received official notice of his discharge from the commission. Early in 1850, he and Condé agreed that, because of "the present condition of California," the survey should be discontinued at the Colorado River and resumed in November at El Paso.

Emory, acting in Weller's place pending the arrival of another commissioner, had no more success getting money than Weller, and in the late spring of 1850 he departed for Washington to press his case. Here he found funds already on the way, but here too the Bureau of Topographical Engineers ended his detail to the boundary survey.

Before leaving California, Emory had dispatched part of the survey contingent under Lieutenant Whipple on a journey by way of Panama and New Orleans to El Paso, where he was to meet General Condé and the new American commissioner in November. The remainder of the party he left in California under Captain Hardcastle, who with a Mexican group under Captain Francisco Jiménez was charged with completing the boundary determination and constructing monuments to mark it.

With funds now forthcoming, Hardcastle and Jiménez prosecuted the task quickly and accurately. Two parties worked toward each other from the extremeties of the line. When their surveys finally met in September 1851, they were so close together that even today no major error is to be found in their work. It was a striking tribute to the ability and dedication of engineers laboring with delicate instruments under unfavorable conditions of climate and terrain.

The Rio Grande Frontier, 1852–53

The reorganized Joint Boundary Commission that met at El Paso in November 1850, with John Russell Bartlett now holding the appointment of United States commissioner, was immediately paralyzed by the furor touched off by his compromise with General Condé. Only a political decision could free the survey to proceed with the boundary from the Rio Grande to the Colorado, and this would not be forthcoming until the spring of 1854, when the United States and Mexico ratified the Gadsden Treaty. In the meantime, the only segment of the frontier on which field parties could constructively operate lay on the Rio Grande between its mouth and El Paso. This work fell to Major Emory, reassigned to the survey in September 1851.

Emory reached El Paso on November 25, 1851. With Bartlett absent on his Mexican adventure, which still had nine months to run, there was no money. The commission had spent half a million dollars and accomplished no more than some preliminary work on the compromise line. Worse yet, the commission was organized, as Emory noted, "on a scale preposterous in magnitude and absurd in principle . . . oppressed with a multitude of officers, quartermasters, commissaries, paymasters, agents, secretaries, sub-secretaries—all officers wholly unknown to any well regulated surveying corps." Emory reduced organization to a semblance of order, equipped three field parties on credit, and turned to the Rio Grande below El Paso.

On its face the task seemed simple enough. According to the Treaty of Guadalupe Hidalgo, the boundary would begin in the Gulf of Mexico three leagues from the mouth of the Rio Grande and follow the deepest channel of the river upstream to the point where it struck the southern boundary of New Mexico north of El Paso. All that needed done was to trace the deepest channel accurately on a series of maps. On its lower reaches the river presented no problem. Between El Paso and Laredo, however, it lay through an unexplored country combining some of the most forbidding mountains, canyons, and deserts in North America. Defining the deepest channel here turned out to be a daunting task.

Beginning about ninety miles below El Paso, the Rio Grande entered the first of a chain of canyons extending with few interruptions nearly to Laredo. They made it difficult and in places impossible to conduct the survey by following the course of the river. Emory therefore selected several points on the river that could be reached by wagon to serve as astronomical observatories and supply depots. At each observatory, Emory himself made the astronomical readings and computed the latitude and longitude. His field parties, under the direction of assistants, then connected these points by lineal survey.

Four of the primary stations were located near El Paso del Norte, where an American town named simply El Paso was taking root on the north side of the river opposite the old. The most important station was at a place called Frontera eight miles north of town, near the initial point of the Disturnell Treaty line. The others were near the cathedral in the plaza of El Paso del Norte, at San Elizario farther downstream, and at the entrance to the first canyon below the valley. All these points were determined by lunar observations as well as by the "beautiful and accurate mode" of "flashes of gunpowder simultaneously observed." Aided by Major Salazar, Mexican commissioner since the death of General Condé in December, Emory passed the first six months of 1852 determining the latitude and longitude of the stations in the El Paso Valley.

From El Paso, in July 1852, Emory moved to the Mexican town of Presidio del Norte, at the confluence of the Rio Grande and Rio Conchos, and set up his instruments. Two field parties had been concentrated to survey the river above and below the astronomical station there.

Discontent over the mounting arrearage in their pay pushed the men to the brink of mutiny.

"On one occasion," wrote Emory, "I was obliged to put down a riot in my camp, single-handed, and at the risk of being shot by an insubordinate fellow, insane from the effects of the intoxicating mezcal."

Happily, a courier dispatched to intercept the San Antonio-El Paso mail brought back an order from the Secretary of the Interior authorizing Emory to draw funds against the department. In another stroke of good fortune, a freight train passing through Presidio del Norte en route from Chihuahua to San Antonio carried five thousand dollars in specie, which the proprietor exchanged for the government draft. Emory paid off his men and discharged the trouble makers.

On August 1, 1852, Salazar and the Mexican surveyors rode into Presidio del Norte. But they were even more inadequately financed than the Americans and unable to match the pace set by Emory.

At the end of August, therefore, Emory pressed the survey independently of Salazar. At the next primary station, Fort Duncan at Eagle Pass, the major set up his instruments to determine latitude and longitude.

The field parties, meantime, remained at Presidio del Norte. Maurice von Hippel supervised the work above Presidio, M. T. W. Chandler, son of a Whig congressman, the work below Presidio. Chandler got himself into some of the most hostile country in the American West.

Below Presidio the Rio Grande described a great arc embracing a wild jumble of mountain and desert later partly included in Big Bend National Park. In three places the river flowed through gigantic canyons with sheer rock walls rising directly from the water's edge. Simply to stay alive in this desolate country, infested with Comanches and Apaches traveling the plunder trails to Mexico, taxed all the resources of mule-mounted explorers. To survey it in addition proved next to impossible.

The Chandler party had to detour entirely around Santa Elena Canyon on the Mexican side, approaching it only at one or two points and looking down at the river from the canyon rim. Below Santa Elena, they made their way slowly down the river as it meandered through a broad valley toward Mariscal Canyon.

Across the river, on the American side, the Chisos Mountains loomed as a landmark for several days. A peak towering above all others afforded a point on which the surveyors repeatedly aligned their instruments. Chandler named it Mount Emory.

While part of the group detoured with the pack train, Chandler took the rest in crude rubber boats down Mariscal Canyon. Rapids wrecked one, and here as in the other canyons he had to content himself with carrying the line no closer than the bordering heights. Beyond Mariscal lay the ruins of the old Spanish presidio of San Vicente, and beyond them still another gorge—Boquillas Canyon. The party had almost reached the limits of endurance, and no relief seemed in sight.

> There is no verdure to soften the bare and rugged view [wrote Chandler]; no overhanging trees or green bushes to vary the scene from one of perfect desolation. Rocks are here piled one above another, over which it was with the greatest labor that we could work our way. The long detours necessarily made to gain but a short distance for the pack-train on the river were rapidly exhausting the strength of the animals, and the spirit of the whole party began to flag.

The loss of the boats, with provisions and clothing, had reduced the men to the shortest rations, and their scanty wardrobes scarcely afforded enough covering for decency. The sharp rocks of the mountains had cut the shoes from their feet, and blood, in many instances, marked their progress through the day's work. Beyond the Sierra Carmel the river seemed to pass through an almost interminable succession of mountains; cañon succeeded cañon; the valleys, which alone had afforded some slight chances for rest and refreshment, had become so narrow and devoid of vegetation that it was quite a task to find grass sufficient for the mules.

At the entrance of Boquillas Canyon, Chandler called off the survey. The party circled south of the Sierra del Carmen through Coahuila and late in November arrived, in destitute condition, at Fort Duncan (Eagle Pass), where Emory was busily engaged in computing latitude and longitude.*

In December 1852, shortly after Bartlett finally met up with Emory at Ringgold Barracks (Rio Grande City), the boundary commission was disbanded as a result of the congressional prohibition of further spending until the Bartlett-Condé compromise was disavowed. Emory repaired at once to Washington, where he found that Congress had relented so far as to authorize the completion of the river survey below the disputed territory. Another commissioner, Robert B. Campbell, replaced Bartlett, but again Emory actually planned and supervised the operation. Work resumed in March 1853.

While Emory himself made the observations at the remaining primary stations—Ringgold Barracks and the mouth of the Rio Grande—and oversaw the routine operation in the lower valley, Lieutenant Nathaniel Michler finished the survey abandoned by Chandler the previous November at San Vicente. His adventures in the canyon country proved equally exciting. While part of the group managed the mule train, the

*Santa Elena, Mariscal, and Boquillas are modern names for these canyons. Chandler, repeating the names by which they were known to local Mexicans, called them, respectively, Cañon Bofecillos, San Carlos Cañon, and "Cañon below Sierra del Carmel." Chandler's Sierra del Carmel, extending deep into Mexico, are known today on the American side as Sierra del Carmen and on the Mexican side as Sierra Encantada.

rest sped down the river in boats. On the first day out from San Vicente, in Boquillas Canyon, Michler revealed himself no better navigator than Chandler:

> After having descended the river for a few miles an immense rapid presented itself to our view. The river here narrowed from nearly three hundred feet to the width of twenty-five; both shores could be touched with the ends of the oars; an immense bowlder divided the main into two smaller channels, leaving but a narrow chute for the boats to descend. The bottom was covered with large rocks, and over these the whole mass of water rushed, foaming and tumbling in a furious manner; a dangerous rapid was thus formed for several hundred feet in length, extending from bank to bank. The two skiffs made the descent in safety, although the waves rolled so high that each plunge filled them almost to overflowing. The flatboat was not so fortunate; totally unmanageable, she ran square against the rocky walls, splintering and tearing away her entire front; such was the force of the blow that the crew were knocked flat on their backs, and the boat-hooks left firmly imbedded in the crevices of the rocks. Thrown back by the great swell, she commenced floating stern foremost down the rapid, gradually sinking. The men stuck to her faithfully, and the skiffs were put into immediate requisition; but by the expert swimming of two of the men, both Mexicans, who had dashed into the current ere the sound of the crash had died away, and seized her lines, she was landed on the end of a sand-bar which most providentially lay at the foot of the rapid; a few feet further, both men and boat would have been destroyed, and our all—provisions and ammunition—irrecoverably lost, the perpendicular banks offering no foothold where to land. With means at hand to repair the wreck, we were again afloat the following day, our craft bereft of all her fair proportions.

By December 1853, the Rio Grande boundary had been explored and mapped from El Paso to the Gulf of Mexico and, with the help of the U.S. Coast and Geodetic Survey, carried three leagues to sea as required by treaty. Major credit for this achievement clearly rested with William H. Emory, whose drive and ability had pushed the work to completion. The Washington politicians had at last learned a lesson. Only six months later, when the Gadsden Purchase Treaty defined a boundary from the Rio Grande to the Colorado, they turned to Major Emory. This time he had no politically appointed superior to complicate the task, for in him alone President Franklin Pierce lodged the three posts of commissioner, surveyor, and chief astronomer. On the Mexican side, Emory's old friend Major Salazar received a similar inclusive appointment. Together the two engineers efficiently and expeditiously filled in the final gap in the international boundary.

The Gadsden Purchase Line, 1854–56

The Gadsden Treaty defined the new boundary precisely, with nothing left to later interpretation, and thus insured against contention such as had confused the marking of the boundary work under the Treaty of Guadalupe Hidalgo. Beginning on the Rio Grande at parallel 31° 47', the line would run due west for one hundred miles, then turn south to parallel 31° 20', then west again to the intersection of this parallel with the 111th meridian, then in a straight line to a point on the Colorado River twenty miles south of its confluence with the Gila, and finally up the middle of the Colorado to the intersection with the line already established between the Colorado and the Pacific. Full power was vested in the two boundary commissioners, whose determination of the line would be final.

Emory and Salazar planned to work from both ends of the line toward the center. One party, under Lieutenant Michler, sailed for San Diego by way of Panama, then marched to Fort Yuma at the mouth of the Gila, arriving on December 9, 1854. Emory himself led the other party, which sailed to Indianola, Texas, and traveled overland to El Paso, where he met Salazar, his counterpart, early in December 1854. Michler's group numbered four officers, twenty hired men, and an escort of sixty soldiers; Emory's three officers, seventy men, and sixty soldiers.

North of El Paso the two teams set up astronomical stations on the Rio Grande and began lunar observations to determine the point where parallel 31° 47' struck the Rio Grande. Within a month this task had been finished.

On January 31, 1855, the military and civil officers of the two commissions gathered at the initial point and signed a paper, one copy in English, the other in Spanish: "We, the undersigned, have this day assembled to witness the laying of the foundation of the monument which is to mark the initial point of the boundary between the United States and the Republic of Mexico, on the part of the United States by William Helmsley Emory, and on the part of the Republic of Mexico by José Salazar y Larregui, latitude 31° 47'." The documents were sealed in a bottle and sunk beneath five feet of earth. Over the spot a stone mason began constructing the initial monument of the Gadsden Treaty line.

Between the initial point and the 111th meridian at Los Nogales Spring, Sonora, Emory's party ran the boundary without Salazar's participation. The revolutionary turmoil in Mexico that unseated Santa Anna later in 1855 caught the Mexican commissioner in a suspected identification with the discredited dictator. A brief time in prison purged him of suspicion, and he returned to his duties in August. In his "unavoidable absence," as the commission journal delicately phrased it, Salazar had agreed to endorse the line as marked by Emory, for Mexico was anxious to complete the work and draw the final payment of $3 million.

The only critical survival problem the surveyors faced on this portion of the boundary was the scarcity of water. Primary astronomical stations had to be established at springs or water holes that were not always convenient to the line, and the readings then had to be transferred to the line by direct measurement or triangulation. These stations were in the Carrizalillo Hills west of present Columbus, New Mexico; at El Espía on the Rio Casas Grandes in Chihuahua; at San Luis Spring east of present Cloverdale, New Mexico; at San Bernardino Spring, Arizona; at Santa Cruz, Sonora; and finally at Los Nogales Spring. By June 1855 the line had been completed and monuments erected as far as the 111th meridian near Los Nogales.

Lieutenant Michler's survey of the boundary from the Colorado River to the 111th meridian proved less routine. Arriving at Fort Yuma in December 1854, he found that the journey from New York, and particularly the rough march from San Diego, had badly deranged the surveying instruments. After repairing them as well as available means permitted, he passed the first two months of 1855 surveying the river from Fort Yuma southward. The densely timbered bottomlands made work in the valley impossible, so

the line was carried along the bordering bench-
lands to the vicinity of the initial point twenty
miles downstream, then brought to the river
bank by hacking a line of sight through the trees.
Numerous dust storms slowed the work by making the use of instruments impossible for days at
a time. Michler also found time during these
months to make copious notes on the appear-
ance and customs of the Yuma Indians and to
pass many pleasant hours in the society of the
post commander at Fort Yuma, Major George H.
Thomas.

Michler's troubles had only begun. On
March 4, 1855, he established an observatory on
top of a low knoll near the initial point on the
river and began taking readings for latitude and
longitude. "Our lucky stars did not, however,
prove to be in the ascendancy," he wrote; "first,
clouds obscured them, and then the rising waters
of the Colorado did not leave us long undisturbed."

Heavy rains far up the Gila dumped heavy
flows into the Colorado, and each day the river's
edge advanced closer to the observatory. On
March 19 the instruments had to be moved back
five hundred yards. The next day, according to
Michler's diary:

Compelled again to move the instruments
and carry them up to camp; every slough is
filled, all rapidly rising, and several swim-
ming deep; rafts built to transport the men
over them; all the men in water up to their
breasts, and instruments only kept dry by
being carried on their heads. About noon
all safely in camp; water within fifty feet of
it, and everybody getting ready to leave. At
sunset the river still continues rising, and
gradually approaches camp, but so slowly
that we are still in doubt. At 2 o'clock a.m.,
decided to take to the sand-hills; the long
roll was beaten, the camp struck, the train
loaded, and all moved on the high plain.
Behind us lay a desert of sand forty miles
across, and in front was spread a sheet of
water several miles in breadth. From fifteen
hundred feet the Colorado had widened to
at least five miles.

Almost immediately, the river began to subside,
but not until April 1 had the valley dried enough for
the surveyors to venture back to their observatory.

Meanwhile, the Mexican party designated by
Salazar to work with Michler arrived belatedly in
charge of Captain Francisco Jiménez, the engineer who had cooperated with Captain Hardcastle in marking the southern boundary of

California four years earlier. Jiménez accepted the computations already made by Michler, and by April 10 the two had completed the determination of the latitude and longitude of the initial point. An initial monument was erected on the azimuth of the boundary about three-fourths of a mile east of the river and preparations made to project the line toward the 111th meridian.

The final segment of the boundary lay across some of the most desolate country in North America. Only one spring could be counted on—that at Quitobaquito in present Organ Pipe Cactus National Monument, about midway on the 240-mile line. The other water was collected during rain storms by the natural rock tanks known as "tinajas," but they could not be depended on. For about twenty-five miles east of the Colorado, the line traversed the shifting white sands of the Yuma Desert, then entered a wild plain studded occasionally with jagged mountains. When he finally crossed it some months later, Michler found it "the most dreary and tiresome I have ever experienced:"

> Imagination cannot picture a more dreary, sterile country, and we named it the "Mal Pais" [bad country]. The burnt lime-like appearance of the soil is ever before you; the very stones look like the scoriae of a furnace; there is no grass, and but a sickly vegetation, more unpleasant to sight than the barren earth itself; scarce an animal to be seen—not even the wolf or the hare to attract the attention, and, save the lizard and the horned frog, naught to give life and animation to this region. The eye may watch in vain for the flight of a bird; to add to all is the knowledge that there is not one drop of water to be depended upon from Sonoyta to the Colorado or Gila. All traces of the road are sometimes erased by the high winds sweeping the unstable soil before them, but death has strewn a continuous line of bleached bones and withered carcases of horses and cattle, as monuments to mark the way.

With summer approaching, mosquitoes swarmed in the Colorado Valley, and the Mexican and American surveyors hastily pushed east into the desert. Mules labored to exhaustion trying to pull the heavily laden wagons through the loose sand, and the advance slowed to a crawl. Then reconnoitering parties brought back word that the tinajas did not contain enough water to support

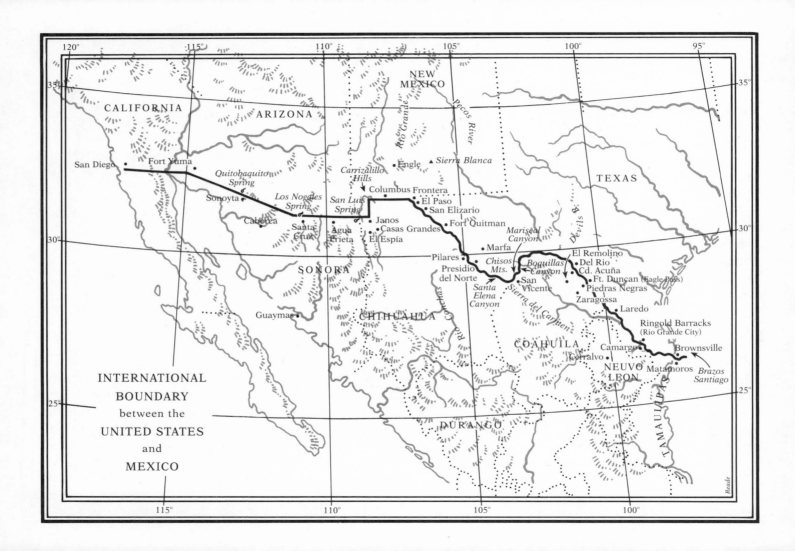

INTERNATIONAL
BOUNDARY
between the
UNITED STATES
and
MEXICO

CALIFORNIA
ARIZONA
NEW MEXICO
TEXAS

San Diego
Fort Yuma
Quitobaquito Spring
Carrizalillo Hills
Engle
Sierra Blanca
Columbus
Frontera
Sonoyta
Los Nogales Spring
San Luis Spring
El Paso
San Elizario
Cabotca
San Luis Spring
Santa Cruz
Agua Prieta
Janos
Casas Grandes
Fort Quitman
El Espía
Marfa
Mariscal Canyon
El Remolino
Del Rio
Cd. Acuña
Pilares
Chisos Mts.
Boquillas Canyon
Ft. Duncan (Eagle Pass)
Presidio del Norte
San Vicente
Piedras Negras
Santa Elena Canyon
Sierra del Carmen
Zaragossa
Laredo
Guaymas
SONORA
CHIHUAHUA
COAHUILA
Ringold Barracks (Rio Grande City)
Camargo
Brownsville
Cerralvo
NEUVO LEON
Matamoros
Brazos Santiago
DURANGO
TAMAULIPAS

Rio Grande
Pecos River
Devils R.
Rio Conchos

Reade

the advance. Reluctantly Michler and Jiménez suspended operations and journeyed by way of the Gila River and Tucson to Los Nogales, where they met Emory late in June.

By now the Sonoran rainy season had set in, and the tinajas could be expected to supply water for field parties. On June 26 Michler and Jiménez began running the boundary westward toward the Colorado. Michler and a small group worked the line while Jiménez and another went ahead to the spring at Quitobaquito to set up a primary astronomical station and compute its latitude and longitude. The survey required all summer, but the rains provided sufficient water to make the operation routine if disagreeable.

Salazar conferred with Emory at El Paso in August, conducted his own survey of the boundary as far as the 111th meridian, then repaired to Janos, Chihuahua. From there, on October 15, 1855, he sent to "Señor Don W. H. Emory" word that "Lieut. Michler has just handed me, in person, an official note, by which I am informed that the topography of the line between meridian 111° and the Colorado is completed." And to his own government he hastened the long-

Opposite: *The boundary in 1856.*

awaited news that "it now only remains for the government of the United States to fulfill its part of the obligations imposed by the 3d article of the treaty [\$3 million]. God and Liberty."

As Emory viewed it, however, there was one more task—completing and signing the maps. He strongly urged that Mexico not be paid until this was done. But the Attorney General of the United States ruled that the termination of field work met the conditions fixed by the treaty, and, in four installments between February 7 and April 4, 1856, the United States made final payment to Mexico for the Gadsden Purchase. Thus, after eight years, the international boundary was at last established and marked in its entirety.*

*Emory received a brevet of lieutenant colonel for distinguished services as boundary commissioner and was appointed a full major of the newly organized First Cavalry in 1855. He continued to preside over the office of the boundary commission in Washington, D.C., until the maps were completed and signed and the voluminous report published. He served as a Union major general in the Civil War and retired in 1876 a regular army brigadier general. He died in 1887.

Printed in the Emory report was a large folded "Map of the United States and their Territories between the Mississippi and the Pacific Ocean and Part of Mexico," prepared by the boundary commission to present an over-all

The marking proved less than permanent. Laborers had accompanied the surveyors to erect boundary monuments, some of dressed stone and others merely piles of rock. Indians destroyed most of these within a few months. At first this made little difference, but as settlers moved west in mounting numbers the land boundary became the focus of property disputes and law and customs enforcement problems. A convention concluded between the United States and Mexico in 1882 and renewed in 1889 called for a resurvey and remarking of the boundary.

With Jacobo Blanco representing Mexico and Lieutenant Colonel John W. Barlow the United States, work commenced in 1892 and was

view of its own work as well as other reliable mapping of the time. By far the most accurate and detailed map of the West yet to appear, it was almost immediately, in 1859, eclipsed by Lieutenant G. K. Warren's monumental map of the Trans-Mississippi West executed for the Pacific Railway Survey. This map drew together the results of the railway surveys and all other mapping that preceded it. In addition to the large map, Emory's office produced a series of fifty-four sectional maps at 1:60,000 tracing the boundary in detail from the Gulf to the Pacific. These were the maps that were ultimately signed by Emory and Salazar as the definition of the boundary called for by the Gadsden Treaty.

completed in 1895. The commission repaired such of the original monuments as still stood and installed new ones where the old had vanished.

Monuments No. 1 and 258 received special attention. Emory and Salazar had erected No. 1 on the Rio Grande north of El Paso in 1855. Of cut stone, it stood 12 feet high, 5 feet square at the base, and 2½ feet square at the top, with inscriptions on the north and south faces. The Barlow-Blanco Commission constructed a cement mortar jacket to protect the foundation stone from flood waters, repointed the joints, and surrounded the site with an iron fence. The opposite end of the land boundary, three miles south of San Diego, had been marked with a cairn of rocks in 1849, but in 1851 Captain Hardcastle had a marble shaft shipped around the Horn and installed in its place. Barlow and Blanco found this monument so mutilated by souvenir hunters that they had it dismantled and restored by a marble firm in San Diego. It was then remounted and surrounded by an iron fence. No's. 1 and 258 stand today as historic edifices in their own right as well as monuments to the achievements of those who surveyed and marked the international boundary, United States and Mexico.

Survey monument marking the point at which the Rio Grande boundary departs from the west bank at El Paso and progresses westward to the Pacific.

The Pacific end of the boundary, marked by a survey monument just south of San Diego.

Border Violence

3

FOR THREE DECADES AFTER THE WAR OF 1846–48, MEXICANS AND Americans menaced each other across the international boundary, and episodes of violence occurred repeatedly to aggravate relations already embittered by the war and its aftermath of boundary disputes. Indian and bandit raids, smuggling activity, revolutionary disturbance, and filibustering expeditions plagued the border throughout the 1850s. With the onset of the 1860s, civil war on one side of the line and attempted foreign conquest on the other fanned the discord. And from 1867 to 1879 the worsening Indian situation goaded the United States into repeated boundary violations that drove the two nations once more to the brink of war.

For Mexico, these were troublous times internally as well. Revolutions, counter-revolutions, and coups produced chronic governmental instability, which in turn contributed to lawless and chaotic conditions on the Mexican side of the border and also invited aggressions from Yankee freebooters infesting the American side. National politics in both countries formed a backdrop to the unfolding history of border violence.

Mexican Politics, 1848–1911

The Mexican-American War left Mexico weak and divided, with the states going their own ways and the impotent and bankrupt central government powerless to impose national authority. Conservatives backed by the army and the church governed precariously. Liberals trumpeting the national humiliation of the war with the United States called on the oppressed and landless to overturn the established order. Driven to the wall, the Conservatives once more summoned Santa Anna to the presidency in 1853. With army support, he set up a corrupt and despotic dictatorship and, selling the Gadsden Purchase area to the United States, added still more to Mexican humiliation. But a growing opposition knocked the props one after another from beneath his regime, and in August 1855 "His Most Serene Highness" fled into exile for the last time.

La Reforma, the Liberal program, promised much but delivered little. It promised an end to the special position in national affairs of the church and the army, and it promised land for the landless. The constitution of 1857 instituted much of the program as the law of the land, but the Liberals lacked the unity to give it much actual effect. The Indian leader of the revolt against Santa Anna, Juan Álvarez, was installed as president in 1855, but he gave way within months to Ignacio Comonfort, a moderate of limited talent whose tendency to appease the Conservatives angered the militant wing of the Liberals. The crisis came in 1858 when the president tried to meet army demands for a more conservative constitution without alienating his Liberal supporters. He pleased neither and hastily repaired to the United States for an extended vacation. General Félix Zuloaga assumed the presidency, and the outraged Liberals withdrew to Querétaro to set up their own congress and executive. Mexico now had two governments.

The new Liberal president was Benito Juárez, a full-blooded Indian who resembled Abraham Lincoln in many traits and today occupies an equally honored place in the history of his nation. He had been in the front ranks of the Liberal movement from the first, and now, at the head of the revolutionary government, he led the Liberal forces in a three-year war against the old order. Enjoying broad support from the masses, he finally prevailed and in 1861 seated himself in the presidential palace in Mexico City.

Juárez occupied the palace for only two years. No sooner had he set about consolidating his regime than the shadow of Europe darkened Mexico. France, England, and Spain joined to force Mexico to pay its debts. England and Spain backed out on discovering that the French emperor Napoleon III had imperial designs on Mexico, but the armies of France alone drove victoriously through the Juáristas and in June 1863 took possession of Mexico City. The president fled, and Austrian Archduke Maximilian, backed by French bayonets, accepted the

Benito Juárez, revered president of Mexico after whom Cuidad Juárez was named.

Porfirio Díaz, who ruled Mexico from 1876 until the revolution of 1911.

"call" to the Mexican throne. For four years Juárez kept alive the resistance movement. For Napoleon, as a result, the Mexican satellite proved an expensive responsibility. When the United States, its own civil war ended, made plain that France must recede from the Western Hemisphere or deal with the victorious armies of the Union, Napoleon abandoned his luckless Austrian puppet, who fell before a Juárista firing squad.

Juárez moved back into the palace in July 1867. With victory complete, however, his followers began to quarrel among themselves, and his power base dissolved swiftly. He clung to the presidency through elections in 1867 and 1871, although after the latter he had to suppress a revolution, and he died in 1872.

Sebastián Lerdo de Tejada succeeded Juárez, but the man of the hour was strongman Porfirio Díaz, Liberal general who had engineered the military triumph over Maximilian and who had instigated the revolution against Juárez in 1871. Díaz organized another revolution and in 1876 drove Lerdo into exile.

Although posing as a Liberal and in fact instituting limited reforms, Díaz ruled for thirty-six years with a heavy and often oppressive hand. At the same time, however, his presidency was a period of unprecedented order, stability, and continuity in domestic and foreign affairs. Foreign capitalists, chiefly American, found the president an agreeable man to do business with, and in large numbers they moved in to exploit the resources of Mexico to their own immense profit and to the financial integrity of the Díaz regime. Relations with the United States improved, and the countries progressed toward an amicable adjustment of boundary problems.

The years of the most serious border violence coincided with the years of civil war and revolution that rent Mexico before the accession of Díaz. During this period Juárez fought to establish himself over the counterforces of reaction, foreign colonialism, and finally opposition within his own camp. Not surprisingly, this was also an unsettled time along the international frontier. The government was preoccupied with more pressing affairs than controlling its people on the boundary and standing firm against American boundary aggressions. Díaz, by contrast, stabilized the boundary as he stabilized the interior. Not until his overthrow in 1911 and the resumption of political chaos in Mexico did the boundary again experience comparable violence.

The Indian Problem, 1848–61

Overbearing Anglo-Americans and resentful Mexicans caused trouble enough along the boundary without the intervention of a third people. But Indians residing on both sides of the line contributed their share to the already unhappy conditions of the boundary country. Mexicans bore the brunt.

For a century or more before the treaties of 1848 and 1853 traced new boundaries, tribes from the north had regularly and systematically ravaged the settlements and haciendas of northern Mexico. From the Great Plains, Kiowas and Comanches scourged the Texas frontier and raided deep into Tamaulipas, Nuevo Leon, Coahuila, Chihuahua, and even remote Durango. From the Sierra Blanca of New Mexico and the mountains bordering the Gila River farther west, Apaches tore up the roads and towns of Chihuahua and Sonora. Stock, plunder, and captives by the hundred, who were integrated into the tribes, enriched these Indians. For all, the raiding pattern was a deeply entrenched cultural feature of economic and social significance. It was not to be surrendered merely because some treaties clothed it with international significance as well.

Article 11 was the one clear gain for Mexico that the negotiators at Guadalupe Hidalgo embedded in the peace treaty of 1848—or so it seemed. The North Mexican states had insisted on it, and the United States agreed for reasons of humanity as well as expediency. Article 11 bound the United States to prevent its Indians from raiding in Mexico, to rescue and return to their homes all Mexican captives held by the tribes, and to enact certain laws in support of these engagements.

The authorities in Washington lacked even a dim understanding of the magnitude of the commitment they had made. The task turned out to be entirely beyond the capabilities of the U.S. Army and the Bureau of Indian Affairs, especially within the financial limits imposed by Congress. The national legislators consistently refused, on economic grounds, to augment these agencies even though the territorial acquisitions of the Mexican-American War had vastly enlarged their responsibilities. The tribes that customarily raided in Mexico numbered about thirty thousand people, yet there were rarely more than three thousand soldiers and a dozen Indian agents in the entire Southwest, including Texas. They could not even prevent incursions on the frontier settlements of Texas and New Mexico, much less bar the warriors from Old Mexico.

The failure stemmed from lack of means, not lack of will. The army built forts along the lower Rio Grande, in southern New Mexico, and later in the Gadsden Purchase. Conscientiously the troops tried to live up to the treaty, but there simply were not enough, especially cavalry, to do it.

Agents of the Indian Bureau also tried hard. In councils with the Indians they demanded, threatened, cajoled, and persuaded, but the tribesmen knew that the government lacked the military strength to enforce its will. With perhaps two dozen exceptions, they refused to surrender the Mexican captives, who usually did not want to be liberated anyway. And although the Indians solemnly signed treaties with the United States promising never again to raid in Mexico, they drew their presents and set forth to raid in Mexico.

American officials sometimes accused Mexico of leaving the entire defense problem to the

United States and thus forfeiting her rights under Article 11, but this was not true. In the first postwar years, the Mexican effort rivaled the American effort.

Beginning in 1848, following Spain's strategy of a century earlier, Mexico laid down a chain of eighteen military colonies along the boundary from the Gulf of Mexico to the Pacific Ocean. Distributed among them, 2,500 soldier-settlers colonized the frontier and sought to defend it against Indians. They did good service, but in the end their labors proved as ineffective as the American. The failure sprang from the national political unrest of the 1850s, the poverty of the frontier country, epidemics of disease, the disruptive effects of the California gold strikes, and the rise of Anglo-American filibustering incursions.

Mexican records, sketchy at best, hint at the magnitude of the Indian menace. Between 1848 and 1853 alone, the official documents and newspapers of Tamaulipas, Nuevo Leon, and Coahuila record casualties of 385 citizens killed, 221 wounded, and 113 carried into captivity. They also chronicle raids that entailed uncounted additional losses. Chihuahua suffered more than

its eastern neighbors but provided no statistics. Sonora, where the impact was well documented, logged human losses in these years of 840 killed, 97 wounded, and 89 taken prisoner. From the observations of Americans who visited the Indians in their home villages, it is certain that the Mexican loss in horses, mules, and cattle amounted to several thousand head each year. Not counted, of course, was the terror and insecurity that constantly gripped the people of the frontier states. Mexicans had good reason to resent the failure of the United States to live up to Article 11 of the peace treaty.

As American officials in the Southwest began to gain knowledge of the strength and capabilities of the Indians, the immensity of the obligation assumed at Guadalupe Hidalgo dawned on policy makers in Washington. Furthermore, the avalanche of Mexican protests falling on the State Department was embarrassing, and when the protests began to arrive with damage claims attached, the embarrassment turned to alarm.

Although the Americans consistently refused to admit any financial liability for Indian damages in Mexico, the troubling fact remained that the United States had solemnly promised to keep the Indians out of Mexico and had dramatically failed. In 1852 diplomats tried to buy release from the commitment, but Mexico's calculation of a fair price of $40 million seemed extravagant. When James Gadsden went to Mexico City a year later, the Indian question was high on his list of items for discussion. It figured prominently in his negotiations, and it found its way into the comprehensive settlement written into the Gadsden Treaty. General Gadsden purchased not only a sizable Mexican acreage but also release from the vexatious Article 11.

The release may have eased the American conscience, but it had no effect on the raiding habits of the Indians. Their destructive forays continued unabated for many years after the Gadsden Treaty. In the late 1850s the U.S. Army scored some signal victories over the Kiowas and Comanches as well as the Apaches. But these successes produced no lasting effect, and the withdrawal of the federal garrisons at the onset of the Civil War in 1861 removed what little restraint they exerted.

Moreover, the warriors perceived that the international boundary could be used to advantage. From Mexican refuges—and with Mexican encouragement, some Americans charged—raiding parties darted across the line, struck at ranches and travel routes, and swiftly withdrew south of the boundary, where pursuers were not supposed to follow. That they sometimes did follow was to cause serious border tensions in the future.

Filibusters and Adventurers, 1848–60

In American history, the decade of the 1850s was the golden age of filibustering. The "manifest destiny" of Anglo-Americans to spread over the continent and perhaps even the hemisphere afforded an altruistic cloak for the mercenary objectives of the typical filibustering expedition. Often it was a genuine cloak, for filibusters easily rationalized themselves as advance agents of their nation's divinely ordained destiny to absorb weaker neighbors and extend over them the blessings of democracy.

Neutrality laws prohibited soldiers of fortune from using United States soil as a platform for the armed invasion of a friendly neighbor.

But the public opinion of the 1850s weakened enforcement of these laws. Many newspapers, a vocal segment of the public, and even high government officials condoned filibustering expeditions. The most notable were launched by Narciso López against Spanish Cuba and by William Walker against Nicaragua. Both ended, as most did, in front of a firing squad. With powerful elements in the United States openly coveting still more Mexican territory, Mexico offered an especially tempting filibustering target.

California and Texas afforded the principal bases. For the California filibusters, the mines of Sonora were the main attraction. The most persistent of those operating from California was a French nobleman, Count Gaston Raousset de Boulbon, who between 1852 and 1854 organized three separate ventures in Sonora. The climax came in August 1854 when he and a small following tried to storm the defenses of Guaymas. The attack foundered and the force fell apart. Sonoran officials terminated the troublesome Frenchman's career with a firing squad.

For William Walker, later to become "prince of filibusters," Lower California was a training ground for the Nicaraguan undertaking of 1855–60. In the autumn of 1853 he and a band of less than fifty men set sail down the coast and put in at La Paz, capital of Lower California. Imprisoning the governor, Walker proclaimed the Republic of Lower California while his men looted the town. Returning up the coast, the adventurers landed at Ensenada, about fifty miles south of the border, and formed a government with Walker as president. Mexican troops from the nearby military colony of Santo Tomás nearly drove the government into the sea, but prospects revived when reinforcements appeared to swell Walker's army to more than two hundred men. Foraging voraciously on the country, they hardly behaved as beneficent liberators.

Early in 1854 the self-styled president proclaimed the Republic of Sonora, annexed it to the Republic of Lower California, and embarked on further conquests. But the citizens, the military, and a famous band of robbers disrupted the march, fragmented the invading force, and ultimately drove it piecemeal across the border into California. U.S. Army officers arrested the "gray-eyed man of destiny," but a jury freed him to fulfill that destiny in front of a firing squad six years later.

The last important California-based expedition was launched in 1857 by Henry A. Crabb. Revolution had broken out in Sonora, with Ignacio Pesqueira attempting to overthrow incumbent governor Manuel Gándara. Crabb thought the revolutionists wanted his aid and ultimately intended to seek the annexation of Sonora to the United States. Forming the "Arizona Colonizing Company," he placed himself at the head of nearly one hundred men and early in 1857 marched overland via Fort Yuma to enter Sonora at Sonoyta. By now, however, Pesqueira had won the governorship, and he rallied the state to fend off the Yankee invasion. At Caborca, ninety miles southeast of Sonoyta, the unwary Americans marched into a trap. Taking refuge in a row of adobe houses, they fought off the Mexican forces for ten days until on April 6 the sixty-nine survivors had to surrender. The Mexicans lined up their prisoners and executed all save one, a boy of fourteen.

More serious disturbances occurred at the other end of the boundary, where Texans and Mexicans faced each other in open hostility across the lower Rio Grande. Aside from historic antipathies rooted in the Texas Revolution and the Mexican-American War, Texans found current grievances to make them especially susceptible to the lure of armed aggression against their Mexican neighbors. The raiding activities of Indians based in Mexico was one. The sanctuary Mexico afforded runaway slaves, who escaped across the boundary by the hundreds, was another. And finally, a prohibitive Mexican tariff system had transformed nearly all the American merchants into smugglers who, despite their comfortable profits, bitterly resented the vigor of Mexican customs enforcement.

From the last of these grievances sprang the Merchant's War of 1850–53. The valley merchants (who tended to be smugglers as well) seized on a revolution that erupted in Tamaulipas to redress their perceived wrongs. Prominent among the revolutionists was José María Carvajal, a Mexican born in Texas who had cast his lot with the Texans in 1836 and 1846. The merchants threw financial support to him, and with it he attracted several hundred American adventurers to his cause.

In the autumn of 1850 Carvajal's army opened the rebellion by assaulting and occupying Camargo, then moved to besiege Matamoros.

Here the defending garrison shattered the attack and threw the insurgents back across the Rio Grande. Carvajal next turned to Cerralvo, but after a four-day encounter again withdrew to the American side of the boundary.

Much of his financial backing slipped away when the Mexican authorities eased tariff restrictions and thereby abated the anger of the American merchants. Early in 1852, however, Carvajal led more than four hundred Americans in another attempt to seize Camargo. This offensive failed, as did still another a year later, and Carvajal's rebellion collapsed.

Twice arrested and freed by United States authorities, Carvajal later, under the Liberal regime in Mexico, rose to high rank in the councils of the Tamaulipas government and distinguished himself in the war against the French invaders.

Many of Carvajal's American recruits had a secondary motive for joining his rebellion. It offered a convenient cover for the lucrative activity of recovering runaway slaves. This source of border trouble combined with another, the Texas raids of Mexican Indians, to produce a serious border incident in October 1855.

Pursuing Indian raiders, Captain James Callahan crossed the Rio Grande with three companies of Texas Rangers. Slaves as well as Indians seem to have been the objective, and possibly some vague scheme for seizing territory. At first the Mexicans aided the undertaking, but later they joined with the Indians to fall on Callahan's command. The rangers retreated to Piedras Negras, pillaged and burned it as a measure of "military necessity," then recrossed the Rio Grande under the protection of the U.S. troops at Fort Duncan.

The incident stirred a furor among Texans, who demanded a revenge expedition. The state's governor joined with the federal military commander, however, to condemn the aggression and stand firm against reprisal. Callahan was dropped from the ranger rolls.

Although not strictly a filibustering episode, the Cortinas War of 1859–60 took on many aspects of one, and its central figure was cast in the mold of the typical filibuster. To Americans along the lower valley, Juan Nepomuceno Cortinas was a stock thief and sometime murderer. To the river Mexicans he emerged as a swashbuckling champion of the downtrodden. With his mother and a retinue of admirers, he lived on a ranch near Brownsville.

Cortinas won his Robin Hood mantle on July 13, 1859, when he shot the overbearing marshal of Brownsville and liberated a Mexican prisoner who had been badly treated by the bullying lawman. Two months later Cortinas invaded Brownsville with about forty men, killed four Texans, set free all the prisoners in the city jail, and established headquarters in the recently abandoned barracks of Fort Brown. Influential Mexicans, including Carvajal, persuaded him to evacuate the town, but two days later, on September 30, he issued a proclamation calling on the authorities of Texas to redress the wrongs of the river Mexicans or he would do it himself. Two weeks later, when Brownsville officials refused to free a jailed Cortinas lieutenant, he threatened to burn the town.

The beleaguered Texans organized a twenty-man militia squad dubbed the Brownsville Tigers and set forth to do battle at the Cortinas ranch. The fight had hardly begun, however, when the Tigers panicked, abandoned their positions and a cannon, and hurried back to town. Early in November a force of Texas Rangers hastened to the rescue. In martial qualities, however, they resembled the Tigers, and when they confronted the enemy they suffered the same humiliating fate.

His prestige and ego soaring, Cortinas effectively ruled the lower valley outside Brownsville. He levied contributions and conscripted recruits. Mexicans from across the boundary flocked to his standard.

In December 1859 effective help finally reached Brownsville. Captain John S. (Rip) Ford with 120 experienced rangers and Major Samuel P. Heintzelman with 165 federal regulars swept up the valley and near Rio Grande City drove the rebel force across the river in disorder. Early in 1860, when Cortinas tried to renew the contest, the rangers and regulars twice crossed into Mexico and defeated him.

At this juncture Colonel Robert E. Lee arrived on the scene. Tactfully yet firmly he communicated the substance of his orders to the authorities at Matamoros: If Mexico did not break up Cortinas's band at once, the United States Army would cross the border in force and do the job itself. This had the desired effect, and Cortinas was driven into hiding in the Burgos Mountains. His freebooting career, however, had not ended.

The aggressions of Raousset, Walker, Crabb, Carvajal, Callahan, and Cortinas were the more dramatic manifestations of a phenomenon that kept the border in turmoil throughout the decade before the American Civil War. Uncounted others on a lesser scale added to the ferment, and still more never got beyond the planning stage.

Of the latter, the most ambitious took form in the active mind of the grand old man of Texan independence, Sam Houston. Elected governor of Texas in 1859, he dreamed of conquering northern Mexico with ten thousand Texas Rangers. He even took some preliminary steps, but the Civil War doomed the project.

Aside from boundary disruptions, the chief effect of the Anglo-American incursions was to deepen Mexican suspicion and resentment of the United States and its citizens and thus to push still farther into the future the day when cordial relations might be developed.

The Civil War Years

With the outbreak of the American Civil War, the lower Rio Grande Valley took on great strategic significance. The Union blockade closed most of the Southern ports, and for a time Brownsville-Matamoros was the only entirely open door through which the South could deal with the outside world.

Indeed, Matamoros was to the Confederacy what New York was to the Union. European arms, ammunition, and supplies of every kind passed through it destined for the seceded states, while cotton, the main exportable staple, crossed the Rio Grande en route to Europe and, covertly, the mills of New England. As one observer remarked, on the road to Brownsville "the chaparral would be almost white in places from the lint detached from passing bales." Despite the nonintercourse decrees of the Juárez government, this lucrative commerce flourished throughout the war years—even after the advent of a federal army on the lower Rio Grande.

The French intervention in Mexico brought new complications, for now civil war flared on both sides of the boundary. The Union favored and diplomatically supported Benito Juárez, who in turn pursued policies antagonistic to the Confederacy. The Confederacy in turn, hoping for French recognition, favored the Imperialist cause in Mexico.

Confusion peaked in 1864, as a federal force that had landed at Brazos Santiago contended with Confederate troops around Brownsville. Across the river, where Juan Cortinas now reigned as Liberal governor of Tamaulipas, a French army mounted an offensive against the Juárista forces holding the state. On the one hand, local Confederate officials intrigued with and received arms from the French, while on the other Juáristas crossed the river and skirmished with the Confederates. On one occasion, in the autumn of 1864, units of Cortinas's army fought beside Union troops in a battle with Confederates. The astonished Southerners found among their Yankee prisoners Mexican soldiers wearing the insignia of a Juárista regiment.

The American Civil War ended at Appomattox Court House on April 9, 1865. More than a month later, on May 13, the last battle of the Civil War was fought at Palmito Hill, ten miles east of Brownsville, Texas. Paradoxically, it was a Confederate victory.

Across the river the other civil war seemed to be drawing to a close too. Disorganized and impoverished, the Juáristas had lost nearly every North Mexican city to the Imperialist forces.

But American protests, muted during the Civil War, now began to bombard Napoleon III in stronger language. To buttress them, General Philip H. Sheridan arrived on the lower Rio Grande in June 1865 with fifty thousand battle-hardened Union veterans. He had no patience with the diplomacy of the State Department, and for nearly two years he pursued every means short of actual invasion to intimidate the French and aid the Republicans. Up and down the Rio Grande he "condemned" huge quantities of war material, then let the Juáristas know that these stockpiles would be left unguarded. His saber-rattling demonstrations kept the French constantly off balance and fearful of open intervention.

With Sheridan's help, the Juáristas rallied, and the resistance took on new life. Gradually the French pulled back from the border with its menacing blue wall beyond. At last, in 1867, Napoleon bowed to Juárista bullets and American diplomacy and pulled out of Mexico, leaving the hapless Austrian archduke Maximilian to his fate.

The vital role the United States had played in the reinstatement of Juárez held forth the prospect that the Mexican and North American republics might verge on a friendship unknown in the past. And in fact, one of the principal irritants of the past, the aggressive, jingoistic expansionism of the American people, had subsided; in its place arose a new and more subtle form of expansionism—peaceful penetration through capital investment.

The heyday of economic imperialism came later, in the era of Porfirio Díaz. In the decade preceding his rise, the United States and Mexico slipped into the old enmity. For one thing, the French interlude had left Mexicans with a hatred for all foreigners, including Americans. For another, and more consequential, the 1870s were years of repeated border irritations that wiped out any residue of good will left over from the days of General Sheridan.

Boundary Troubles of the 1870s

Many irritants plagued the border in the decade of the 1870s. Outlaw gangs infested both sides from the Gulf to the Pacific and preyed on the populace of both nations. Texas cattle herds in particular suffered severely from their depredations. A customs-free zone ten miles wide along the Rio Grande in Tamaulipas, established in 1858 to discourage the population exodus to the United States, set the stage for smuggling and other abuses that cost both nations severely in revenue and angered border Americans. Kiowas, Comanches, and Apaches continued to plunder Mexico while Kickapoo, Lipan, Apache, and other formerly American tribes that had moved to Mexico struck in Texas, New Mexico, and Arizona. One Mexican and three American investigating commissions took testimony from border inhabitants in the early 1870s, but their reports were biased and contributed nothing to solving the problems.

The United States considered itself unacceptably victimized by Mexican Indians and outlaws and showed less and less respect for the international boundary. If Mexico would not police her own lawless elements, the United States would do it for her.

The first major incident occurred in the spring of 1873. Visiting Fort Clark, Texas, Secretary of War William W. Belknap and General Philip H. Sheridan orally instructed Colonel Ranald S. Mackenzie to clean out a nest of Kickapoo raiders on the San Rodrigo River about fifty miles west of Piedras Negras. The two officials would not commit the order to writing but promised that President Ulysses S. Grant would support the young colonel if there were repercussions. In response, Mackenzie led his cavalry regiment in a daring thrust into Mexico and on May 18 fell on the Kickapoos at El Remolino. Nineteen Indians were slain and forty women and children seized as prisoners. As angry Mexicans and Indians swarmed on the flanks and rear, the command hastily withdrew across the boundary. Mexico's envoy in Washington protested loudly, but true to his word the president shielded Mackenzie from the disciplinary action demanded by Mexico.

The second boundary incident took place in November 1875, when a force of United States cavalry under Captain James F. Randlett tried to head off a gang of Mexican rustlers. The thieves got across the Rio Grande with their stolen cattle at Las Cuevas, near Camargo, and Randlett demanded that the village alcalde surrender the culprits and return the stock. While Randlett awaited reinforcements to enable him to cross the river and enforce the demand, Captain L. H. McNelly and a detachment of Texas Rangers reached the scene and at once charged into Mexico, where they collided with 250 Mexican regulars. Randlett pushed the United States regulars across to support the hard-pressed Texans, but after a brief exchange of gunfire a truce was arranged. That night, under orders from his superiors, Randlett withdrew his men, and McNelly returned the next morning. Again Mexico forcefully protested this violation of her soil.

In 1876 and 1877 invasion of Mexican territory occurred repeatedly. Acting under orders from General Edward O. C. Ord, Lieutenant Colonel William R. Shafter and his energetic commander of Seminole Indian scouts, Lieutenant John L. Bullis, crossed into Mexico time and again. In July 1876 they surprised a Lipan camp in Coahuila, killed fourteen men, captured ninety-six horses and mules, and destroyed the village. In January 1877 Bullis and his scouts, supported by two hundred cavalrymen, drove 125 miles southward into Coahuila. In March of the same year, Shafter invaded Piedras Negras to free some Mexicans imprisoned for guiding American troops, but the prisoners were spirited out of town before the colonel reached the jail. And in October 1877 Bullis attacked and burned an Indian camp near Zaragoza, nearly clashed with Mexican regulars, and withdrew across the border covered by three hundred troopers ordered to his support by Shafter.

These developments unfolded against a backdrop of governmental change in both countries. In Mexico in 1876 Porfirio Díaz made good his bid for power, in part by inflaming the populace with the issue of American boundary aggressions. In the United States Rutherford B. Hayes assumed the presidency in 1877 determined to withhold recognition from Díaz and pursue a firm Mexican policy until border troubles were brought under control.

Díaz refused to be intimidated. Any concessions to Americans while their troops paraded on Mexican soil would imperil his government. He stood firm by sending a division of regulars to the frontier with orders to shoot any United States soldiers found on the wrong side of the line. But he also intimated that if the two nations could get along better American capitalists might find attractive investment and commercial opportunities in Mexico.

Although war nearly broke out in 1877, by the spring of 1878 the Hayes administration sensed that popular ardor for a belligerent Mexican policy had cooled and granted the recognition Díaz wanted. Still, the United States made clear, friendly relations depended on certain border guarantees, and these Díaz would not yield under the threat of continued officially sanctioned border violations.

For another two years diplomats used blunt language while at the same time American financiers were discovering the lucrative possibilities of which the Mexican strongman had hinted. In the end their influence prevailed. In 1880 President Hayes revoked the army's authority to cross the boundary.

With the United States no longer pursuing a Mexican policy backed by coercion, Díaz turned cooperative. Conventions were negotiated to permit troops of either nation to cross the boundary in pursuit of raiding Indians. Under these arrangements, the United States and Mexican armies prosecuted the final campaigns against the Apaches, last of the rebellious tribes. By 1886 the Indians had been conquered and one of the most persistent and aggravating sources of international friction eliminated.

Pancho Villa and the End of Border Violence, 1914–20

The years from 1880 to 1911 featured unprecedented harmony between the United States and Mexico. The reasons stemmed from the order and stability of Mexico and the deep involvement of Americans in Mexican economic affairs.

Powerful men in the United States had powerful motives for wanting international amity. By 1911 they had built more than ten thousand of Mexico's sixteen thousand miles of railroad, and their holdings were valued at nearly $650 million. By 1911 American mining corporations had Mexican assets of $250 million. American firms acquired and exploited millions of acres of Mexican grass, mineral, timber, farming, and oil lands.

In 1912 American investment in Mexico reached nearly $3 billion, and fifty to seventy thousand Americans resided there. In this year, according to a later Senate committee estimate, Americans owned 78 percent of Mexico's mines, 72 percent of her smelters, 58 percent or her oil, and 68 percent of her rubber.

Against this background, Mexico and the United States speedily reached agreements to resolve long-simmering disputes. Treaties concluded in 1884, 1889, 1905, and 1906 addressed boundary problems, and in 1892 the International Boundary Commission was established as a joint organization charged with overseeing boundary affairs.

As a symbolic expression of the new harmony, in 1909 Presidents Díaz and William Howard Taft met in the center of the international bridge linking El Paso with Juárez. Afterward they held conferences that testified to the spirit of good will that had come to characterize relations between the United States and Mexico.

But foreign economic domination combined with Díaz's repressive rule to produce mounting discontent in Mexico. In the first decade of the twentieth century, abused peasants and Indians and outraged intellectuals began to unite against the dictator. When he sought reelection in 1910, Francisco I. Madero drew together all the diverse elements of the opposition, and in May 1911, after thirty-five years of rule, Porfirio Díaz went into exile.

Once more chaos swept Mexico. The army, the church, and the land barons saw their privileges threatened. Counter-revolution overturned

Madero and in February 1913 installed army chief Victoriano Huerta, who promptly murdered Madero.

Most of the great powers recognized the Huerta government. President Woodrow Wilson, however, introducing a new idealism into international affairs, withheld United States recognition and sought the overthrow of this "desperate brute" in Mexico City. The test of wills between the two men climaxed in an incident at Tampico in April 1914, when Mexican officials seized a U.S. Navy boat crew. The United States demanded forms of apology that Huerta refused to extend, and American troops occupied Vera Cruz. Mediation by Argentina, Brazil, and Chile ended the crisis.

Meanwhile, American opposition to Huerta strengthened his foes. With arms purchased in the United States, Constitutionalists under the leadership of Venustiano Carranza at last, in July 1914, unseated Huerta.

Then the victors fell to quarreling. The chief antagonists were the new president, Carranza, and General Francisco "Pancho" Villa, an unlettered warlord who commanded wide peasant support in Sonora and Chihuahua. Civil war

General Francisco "Pancho" Villa, whose forces plagued both sides of the border from 1915 to 1920.

blazed for a year, but by the spring of 1915 Villa had been eliminated as a serious military threat to the Carranza government. With a bandit army of about five thousand men, however, he continued to run wild in the northern states. From 1915 to 1920 Pancho Villa and his followers brought violence again to the border country.

Villa's anti-American crusade drew on several motives. One was mere plunder. Another was revenge: the United States had let Carranza use the Southern Pacific Railroad from El Paso to Douglas, Arizona, to concentrate his forces against the Villistas, and it was near Agua Prieta, across the border from Douglas, that Villa had lost the decisive battle of the civil war. And finally, Villa hoped to provoke the United States into a retaliation against Mexico that would bring down Carranza. Wilson was not getting along well with Carranza anyway, and Villa's policy nearly succeeded.

Villa's vendetta took its toll of Yankees. In January 1916 Villistas stopped a train at Santa Ysabel, Chihuahua, pulled off seventeen U.S. citizens, and summarily executed sixteen of them.

Three months later Villa forces staged an incident certain to arouse United States fury.

Shortly after midnight on March 9, one thousand of Villa's men charged into the border town of Columbus, New Mexico, held by some two hundred U.S. cavalrymen. Although surprised, the soldiers fought back tenaciously, and gunfire rocked the town through the night. Eighteen Americans, both soldiers and townspeople, were killed and as many wounded. At dawn, with more American cavalry racing to the rescue, the Villistas hastily withdrew, leaving twenty-five to thirty of their own dead in the streets. The relief column, under Major Frank Tompkins, gave chase across the border into Mexico, smashed through three rear-guard defenses, and killed another seventy-five of the raiders. This bold foray had cost Villa heavily, but he had indeed succeeded in provoking the United States.

At once orders from Washington assigned General John J. Pershing to lead an expedition into Mexico to disperse the bandit forces and if possible capture or kill Villa. Supposedly with Carranza's consent, Pershing crossed the border at Columbus six days after the Villa raid and, ultimately with twelve thousand regulars, drove deep into Chihuahua. Wide-ranging cavalry columns scoured the deserts and mountains and occasionally clashed with Villista bands. By late May 1916 Pershing had driven three hundred miles into Chihuahua, nearly to the Durango border, and had slain more than two hundred Villistas.

But he had not captured Villa. Wounded in a fight with Carranzistas on May 27, the bandit leader had gone into hiding, and his army had disintegrated.

In June Pershing pulled back to a point near Casas Grandes, 150 miles south of the boundary. With no organized opposition, he settled into a routine of patrolling the countryside.

Twice Pershing's troops collided with Carranza's troops. This infuriated Mexican opinion and prompted the president to demand the withdrawal of the punitive expedition. President Wilson refused. Carranza then ordered his commanders to shoot at all U.S. columns moving in any direction except north, toward the border. Wilson mobilized the National Guard, two hundred thousand strong, and strung it along the border. The United States and Mexico drifted toward war.

Meanwhile, on the night of May 5, 1916, 115 Villistas—possibly led, paradoxically, by a

General John J. "Black Jack" Pershing, who led 12,000 U. S. troops into Mexico in 1916.

Carranzista colonel—crossed the Rio Grande in the rugged country now included in the Big Bend National Park. Part of the force raided the village of Boquillas, sacked Deemer's Store, and made off with four American captives. The prisoners, however, overpowered their four guards and brought them back to Texas for trial.

The other party of Mexicans assailed and looted the small settlement of Glenn Springs, where a squad of nine soldiers had been posted. Two of the troopers were in their tents and escaped. Of the remaining seven, trapped in an adobe hut with thatched roof, which the Mexicans fired, an observer wrote:

> Three had been killed. Their bodies were found near the building. Pvt. Cohen had jumped from the building, only to have his face blown off. Pvt. Coloe lay about ten feet from the door, and Pvt. Rogers, with his clothes afire, had made an easy target for the Mexicans when they dropped him only 100 yards from the shack. The four remaining soldiers, Sergeant Smythe among them, were in horrible condition with gaping wounds and blisters as large as hen eggs on their bodies. When the Mexicans set fire to the thatched roof, the adobe shack became a man-sized inferno. They were caught undressed and when they made their escape over the burning coals, their bare feet suffered greatly.

In response to the Boquillas and Glenn Springs raids, two troops of cavalry under Colonel George T. Langhorne crossed into Mexico and gave chase, but the raiders scattered. After sixteen days of trailing, the cavalrymen returned to the border.

With Villa's army dispersed, Pershing could accomplish little by remaining in Mexico. Yet to withdraw without guarantees against future raids would be a humiliating confession of failure. Still, when Carranza in July 1916 suggested that the question be negotiated, Wilson readily agreed.

In September 1916 a joint Mexican-American commission met in New London, Connecticut. For four months the diplomats talked. The Americans insisted on commitments from Mexico to protect American lives and property and prevent border depredations. The Mexicans would promise nothing until the Americans agreed to get Pershing out of Mexican territory.

Deadlocked, in January 1917 the commission disbanded.

Now Wilson had the choice of meeting Carranza's demand for Pershing's withdrawal or moving forward with war measures. With the United States drifting into the European war, the president chose the former course. Before the month had ended, the movement was underway, and on February 5, 1917, the last of the punitive expedition crossed the boundary.

Villa's army had been smashed as an organized force, and the bandit chieftain himself menaced the border no more. After Carranza's assassination in 1920, Villa patched up a peace with the successor government and retired to his Parral estate. In 1923 an assassination squad ended his life with forty-seven bullets.

Despite Villa's disappearance from the border, in the months after Pershing's withdrawal swarms of footloose Villistas infested the border country. Occasionally they darted across the line in plundering forays. The Big Bend country of Texas was the principal objective, and Colonel Langhorne's cavalry, with headquarters at Marfa, patrolled this danger zone throughout 1917 and 1918.

Two raids were especially notable. On Christmas morning 1917, a large bandit gang attacked the headquarters of the Lucas C. Brite ranch thirty-five miles west of Marfa. The Brites were in Marfa, but the ranch foreman and his family, with a handful of holiday visitors, successfully defended the Brite home. The bandits pillaged the store, killed the driver and two passengers of a mail hack, and made off with Brite's herd of riding horses.

A neighboring rancher had heard the shooting and telephoned the news to Marfa. By noon dozens of automobiles loaded with ranchmen, cavalrymen, and Texas Rangers were bouncing over the rutted roads from Marfa and Valentine to the Brite ranch. Discovering the approach of this cavalcade, the Mexicans hastily pulled out. As they made their way down the precipitous trail over the Candelaria Rim, where the plateau breaks away to the river bottom, the pursuers came within shooting distance, dropped several of the fugitives, and forced others to abandon some of their loot.

The next day a posse of rangers and soldiers crossed into Mexico and on December 27 assaulted the bandit stronghold of Pilares. Some thirty-five Mexicans were slain and much of the stolen merchandise and stock recovered. Although nearly every man in Pilares was a bandit, not everyone killed by the American posse was in on the Brite raid. The Carranza government protested the killing of innocent townspeople, and the Texas adjutant general opened an investigation that led to the disbanding of the ranger company involved.

The second major raid took place three months later, on March 25, 1918, against the Ed Nevill ranch south of Van Horn. Nevill and his teenage son Glenn raced from the house for the chaparral. Ed made his escape, but Glenn was shot down in the doorway, where his body was later found badly battered with clubs and rifle butts.

Two troops of cavalry promptly took the trail. Again it led to Pilares. The fugitive raiders, heavily reinforced by others from Pilares and also by Carranzista soldiers, set up defenses to receive the invading troopers. The cavalry charged, the defenders gave way, and the fight moved into the town itself, ending with the death of thirty-three Mexicans and one American.

The attack on the Nevill ranch was the last of the big bandit raids. Minor raids now and then disturbed the border country, and the cavalry patrolled the Big Bend well into the 1920s. But as the revolutionary turmoil subsided and the Mexican government established better police control, large-scale border violence ended. Rustling and smuggling continue today, but compared with the border adventures of the Villistas, these are tame pastimes indeed.

The River Frontier

4

THE EMORY-SALAZAR SURVEYS DISCLOSED THAT THE UNITED States and Mexico faced each other across a land frontier of nearly seven hundred miles and a river frontier of more than thirteen hundred miles. Measured by the sinuosities of the Rio Grande, the boundary between its mouth and the initial point of the Gadsden Purchase line totaled thirteen hundred miles. (Later the river rectification program reduced this figure to twelve hundred.) In addition, for about twenty miles below its junction with the Gila, the Colorado formed another segment of the water boundary. Thus the river frontier was almost twice the length of the land frontier.

The river frontier accounted for nearly all the boundary difficulties that plagued the United States and Mexico for more

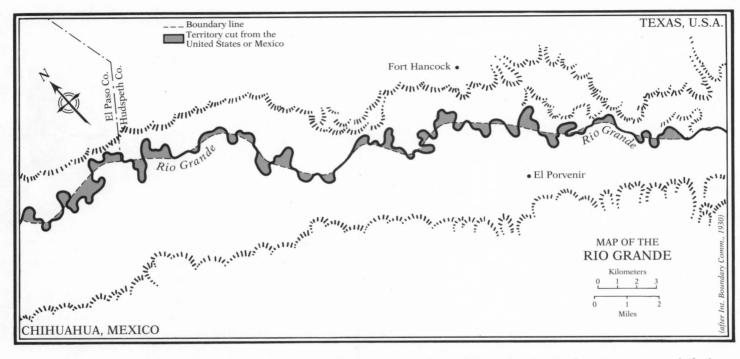

Legend:
- - - - Boundary line
- Territory cut from the United States or Mexico

TEXAS, U.S.A.

El Paso Co.
Hudspeth Co.

N

Fort Hancock •

Rio Grande

Rio Grande

• El Porvenir

MAP OF THE
RIO GRANDE

Kilometers
0   1   2   3

0   1   2
Miles

(after Int. Boundary Comm., 1930)

CHIHUAHUA, MEXICO

Survey maps such as these show the meanderings of the Rio Grande and how the river's changing course shifted land back and forth between the U. S. and Mexico.

than a century. The explanation lay chiefly in the character of the Rio Grande and the Colorado. Before tamed in the twentieth century, both were unruly and unstable rivers. As alluvial streams carrying huge loads of silt, they wandered snake-like across their broad lower valleys, constantly changing course by gradual means (erosion and accretion) and by sudden, violent means (avulsion). Traversing an arid land, they alike gave life to and destroyed their lower basins. In the spring, with the melting of the snowpack in the Rocky Mountains, the Rio Grande and Colorado were wild torrents overflowing and ripping up the floodplain, in the autumn mere trickles of muddy water that in places sank entirely from view. The lower Rio Grande could also run amuck in the summer and autumn months, when tropical storms in the mountains of Mexico flooded the tributaries from which this stretch of the river drew its largest volume.

The instability of the boundary rivers gave rise to varied problems. Their ever-changing course placed the exact location of the boundary frequently in doubt, with consequent uncertainties for property owners, government authorities, and law enforcement officers of both nations. The fluctuating volume of the river raised questions of equitable water distribution and flood control that vitally concerned inhabitants on both sides of the boundary. With the increase of population along the frontiers of Mexico and the United States in the last quarter of the nineteenth century, these became pressing problems of mounting complexity. Only through international cooperation could they be fairly resolved. In the 1880s the two countries made a start. To overcome historic antipathies and wide cultural differences was not easy. Although border violence and boundary disputes continued well into the twentieth century, they were offset and at length overshadowed by the solid results of a growing determination to settle differences amicably and justly. This spirit of cooperation at last, in 1963, attained full maturity with the harmonious resolution of the last important boundary controversy.

The Treaties of 1884 and 1889

As early as 1856, when the Rio Grande still flowed through almost unpopulated country, Major Emory glimpsed the troubles that were certain to develop as more people settled on the river. One of the pioneer founders of the American

El Paso, James Wiley Magoffin, wrote to Emory that the Rio Grande in the El Paso Valley threatened to change its course. What, he asked, would this do to the boundary line so recently surveyed?

Emory referred the question to Washington, where it landed on the desk of Attorney General Caleb Cushing. His lengthy opinion summed up the principles of international law that governed river boundaries. If the river changed its course by the slow and methodical process of erosion of one bank and accretion to the other, then the boundary moved with the deepest channel. If, on the other hand, the river changed its course suddenly by avulsion—if, that is, it deserted its old bed and cut a new one—then the boundary remained in the old bed. Cushing's opinion, which simply restated long-recognized principles, defined the basis for dealing with boundary problems on the Rio Grande and the Colorado.

One after another in the 1860s and 1870s the instances of contested or uncertain sovereignty arising from the peripatetic habits of the Rio Grande intruded on the diplomacy of the United States and Mexico. As early as 1867, in an exchange of correspondence concerning boundary problems in the El Paso Valley, the Secretary of State and the Mexican Minister in Washington expressed agreement with the opinion of Attorney General Cushing. On several occasions in the next decade, diplomats of both governments reaffirmed the agreement.

In 1875 Mexico suggested that the principles stated by Cushing be specifically applied by treaty to the river boundary and submitted a draft accord to the State Department for consideration. Nothing came of the proposal until 1884, when a dispute over Morteritos Island in the Rio Grande near Roma, Texas, precipitated the issue. The testimony of General Emory, now retired, decisively influenced the Morteritos settlement, but Mexico and the United States resolved to go a step further and conventionalize the Cushing opinion, as Mexico had urged ten years earlier. In Washington on November 12, 1884, Secretary of State Frederick Frelinghuysen and Mexican Minister Matías Romero signed the "Convention between the United States of America and the United States of Mexico Touching the International Boundary Line where it Follows the Bed of the Rio Grande and the Rio Colorado."

The Treaty of 1884 provided that the international boundary would forever remain in the middle of the deepest channel of the two boundary rivers. When the river moved, so would the boundary—so long as the move was "effected by natural causes through the slow and gradual erosion and deposit of alluvium and not by the abandonment of an existing river bed and the opening of a new one." If the current cut a new bed or a new deepest channel, however, it would "produce no change in the dividing line as fixed by the surveys of the International Boundary Commission in 1852, but the line then fixed shall continue to follow the middle of the original channel bed, even though this become wholly dry or be obstructed by deposits." The treaty made clear that property rights in and national jurisdiction over enclaves thus thrown by avulsion to the other side of the river were not impaired by their physical attachment to the territory of the neighboring nation.

The treaty also outlawed all human works along the river that tended to produce artificial change in the deepest channel. This was designed to strengthen the provision of the Treaties of 1848 and 1853 for ensuring navigability. No one still seriously intended to navigate the Rio Grande or the Colorado, but the legal fiction was maintained for many years and obstructed for a time the great dam-building programs of the twentieth century.

To commit the principles to paper was one thing, to apply and enforce them another. It was not always apparent whether changes in the river had occurred through erosion and accretion or through avulsion. And even where the natural process of change was clear, the river dwellers whose interests were jeopardized did not hasten to invoke the treaty. Boundary disputes, especially in that perennial locus of dispute the El Paso Valley, continued to find their way into diplomatic channels.

Clearly, some form of machinery to apply the provisions of the Treaty of 1884 to specific situations was badly needed. Again the initiative came from Mexico, and in Washington on March 1, 1889, Minister Romero and Secretary of State Thomas Bayard signed a treaty authorizing the creation of such machinery.

The Treaty of 1889 called for the formation of an International Boundary Commission, United States and Mexico (IBC). Each nation agreed to appoint a commissioner, a consulting engineer, and such staff members as were needed. From headquarters somewhere on the border, the IBC would make on-the-spot investigations of such river changes as came to its attention, decide whether they had been produced by erosion and accretion or by avulsion, and then apply the Treaty of 1884. Works such as diversion dams, jetties, and bridges were also to fall within the purview of the IBC, which could suspend their construction or order their removal if they violated the navigability provisions of the Treaties of 1848, 1853, and 1884. To aid its investigations, the IBC could call on local authorities for papers and information deemed necessary to its duties and could also summon witnesses to testify. When the two commissioners agreed to a decision, it was binding unless specifically disapproved by either or both governments within one month. If the commissioners disagreed, "both Governments shall take cognizance of the matter" and settle it amicably as specified by the Treaty of Guadalupe Hidalgo.

The Treaties of 1884 and 1889 laid the groundwork for the harmonious resolution of boundary difficulties and for the ultimate stabilization of a notoriously unstable frontier. The diplomats who negotiated them hardly foresaw the evolution of the IBC into a unique international organization that, with one conspicuous exception, was to write a near-perfect record in the peaceful settlement of international problems.

The International Boundary Commission

The ratification process took nearly two years and appointment of officials another two. Not until January 8, 1894, did the IBC formally organize in the office of the Mexican consul in El Paso, Texas. From then on, the United States section maintained offices in El Paso, the Mexican section across the river in Ciudad Juárez—the old El Paso del Norte.

As American commissioner, President Grover Cleveland appointed a veteran army officer, Colonel Anson Mills, who was promoted to brigadier general in 1897. Mills's experience with the boundary country dated from 1857, when as

Opposite: *International Boundary Commission map from 1889 of the El Paso-Cuidad Juárez area.*

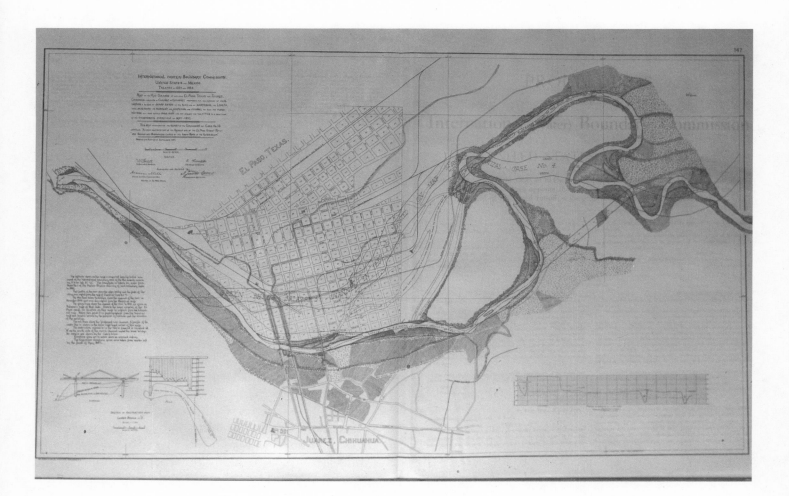

INTERNATIONAL (WATER) BOUNDARY COMMISSION.
UNITED STATES and MEXICO.
TREATIES of 1884 and 1889.

EL PASO, TEXAS.

JUAREZ, CHIHUAHUA.

a youthful surveyor he had tramped the deserts of western Texas and laid out the first plat of the city of El Paso. His twenty-year incumbency on the IBC spanned a period of fruitful activity and ended coincident with revolutionary ferment in Mexico that for a time devitalized the commission.

The first Mexican commissioner, José María Canalizo, died shortly after the organization meeting. His successors during the tenure of Mills were Francisco Javier Osorno (1894–98), Jacobo Blanco (1898–1906), and Fernando Beltrán y Puga (1906–14). All, Mills wrote, were "equal in legal and judicial attainments to similar officials of our own government. They sought always to attain righteous decisions and I think succeeded in the many cases that came before us."

The IBC at once found itself preoccupied with a typical kind of river action to which the Treaty of 1884 clearly applied but to which in practical terms it seemed to have little relevance. This was the formation of tracts of land called bancos, which occurred by the score in the Rio Grande Valley below Rio Grande City and to a lesser extent in the El Paso and Colorado valleys. The river meandered back and forth across the floodplain in a design somewhat like an inter-minable letter S. In successive sweeping bends, the current ate away the unstable concave banks and built up the convex banks. Ultimately it turned on itself and, usually by a sudden (avulsive) breakthrough, carved a new channel across the remaining neck of land. The result was to throw a pear-shaped tract of land, or banco, from one side of the river to the other—from one nation to the other.

The Treaty of 1884 explicitly provided for this contingency. The change having occurred avulsively, the boundary remained in the old river bed, and sovereignty and property rights in the banco remained with the nation from which it had become physically detached.

But the Rio Grande rarely yielded such a stereotyped case. It had a habit of moving away from its new channel into yet newer ones, thus leaving the banco as an enclave of one nation entirely surrounded by the territory of the other. Moreover, the river often cut still more bancos to complicate the original complication. And in time farming obliterated the dry channels where the boundary was supposed to rest. In short, the alluvial valleys were patchworks of bancos and mazes of abandoned river beds that made determination of the boundary a truly formidable undertaking.

The consequences were hardly academic. The pattern of land ownership along the most densely populated and intensively cultivated stretches of the river became terribly confused. Residents of bancos found themselves physically detached from their country of nationality, with attendant complications for them as well as for political authorities on both sides of the boundary. And smugglers and other criminals ran wild because law enforcement officers and the courts were uncertain where the boundary lay.

Shortly after its organization in 1894, the IBC began to investigate four banco cases on the lower Rio Grande that had been persistent local irritants for years. After examining Bancos Carmargo, Vela, Santa Margarita, and Granjeno on the ground and listening to testimony bearing on the time and manner of their formation, Commissioners Mills and Osorno concluded that the principles of the Treaty of 1884 failed to furnish a realistic solution to the banco problem. Both advised their governments that the sovereignty of bancos ought to reside, without alienation of original property rights, in the nation to which

they became physically attached. This would eliminate troublesome foreign inholdings from both countries and place the boundary with few exceptions on the river itself.

In anticipation of a new accord to make this possible, the IBC began surveying and compiling records on all the bancos that would be affected if their recommendations were accepted. It also turned to cases not involving bancos. One, the contested ownership of San Elizario "Island" below El Paso, was decided in favor of the United States in 1896. Another, the dispute over the Chamizal tract in downtown El Paso, raised the one major issue on which the commission could find no mutually acceptable solution.

Still another, the Horcón Ranch case, brought into play the commission's responsibility for artificial changes in the river. Near Brownsville, Texas, the Rio Grande described two loops (see diagram). The American Rio Grande Irrigation Company maintained a pumping station on the upper loop (A), but discovered its operation imperiled as the river threatened to cut through the base of this loop (B) and leave it a dry bed. The company therefore dug an artificial cut (C) that straightened the river and

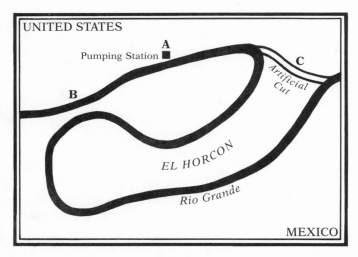

Diagram of the Rio Grande meander in the Horcón Ranch case.

relieved the pressure on B. This action, however, made a dry channel of the lower loop and deprived the Mexican farmers along it of their water supply. In 1906 Mexico brought the case before the IBC, which quickly found the cutoff a clear violation of the Treaty of 1884.

The Horcón case raised the question of the powers of the IBC. The Treaty of 1889 gave it authority to suspend construction of works that violated the Treaty of 1884. But here the change had already been made, and to retrieve it was impracticable. How could the American irrigation firm be compelled to compensate the injured Mexican parties? The answer lay in the courts. In this case the Department of Justice brought suit against the company in the United States District Court at Brownsville. The court found in favor of the United States, and the company paid damages to the landholders who had suffered because of the cutoff. Although the Horcón case represented a victory for the IBC, it also dramatized the limitation on its powers. In other cases the courts were not always so cooperative in upholding and enforcing the commission's decisions.

The Banco Treaty of 1905

Both Washington and Mexico City agreed in principle with the recommendation of their commissioners that bancos ought to be treated in a more practical way than specified by the Treaty of 1884. But the issue required a decade of sporadic negotiation before the two governments could agree on a formula for accomplishing the result. The chief difficulty lay in a provision in the Mexican constitution prohibiting the cession of any part of the national domain. The IBC's recommendation that it be empowered to "announce the transfer of jurisdiction" of bancos would come close, if adopted, to violating the constitution. To satisfy Mexico, the treaty had to avoid the implication that a transfer of territory was involved.

The convention finally concluded in Washington on March 20, 1905, satisfied Mexico, although precisely how remained somewhat vague. The treaty dealt with two classes of bancos—those already surveyed by IBC engineers and those unsurveyed or even yet unformed.

The former class was covered by a report submitted by the IBC in 1898 containing the surveys of fifty-eight bancos between the mouth of the Rio Grande and the mouth of the Rio San Juan, which entered the Rio Grande from Mexico nearly opposite Rio Grande City, Texas. The Treaty of 1905 declared these bancos "eliminated from the effects of Article II of the Treaty of November 12, 1884." Along this stretch of the river, the boundary would follow the deepest channel. "Dominion and jurisdiction" over bancos on the right bank would, by action of the treaty itself, pass to Mexico, while dominion and jurisdiction over those on the left bank would pass to the United States.

The second class of bancos—those surveyed or formed in the future—were to be governed by the same principles. After investigation and survey by the IBC, they too would be "eliminated" from the effects of the Treaty of 1884. If bancos in this category exceeded 250 hectares (617.75 acres) in area or two hundred persons in population, however, they were not to be treated as bancos and would remain as detached areas of the parent nation. In such instances, the abandoned river bed would be marked as the international boundary.

Finally, the Treaty of 1905 preserved all rights of individuals affected by it. Residents of eliminated bancos could keep their old or acquire new citizenship as they desired. Owners of property passing to the neighboring nation could sell or retain it as they wished. Property of all kinds in the bancos would be "inviolably respected," and its owners would "enjoy as complete security with respect thereto as if it belonged to citizens of the country where it is situated."

The first series of fifty-eight bancos having been eliminated by the treaty itself, the IBC at once began to investigate bancos that would make up the second series. By 1912 an additional thirty-one, numbered fifty-nine through eighty-nine, nearly all of which were formed after the survey of 1897–98, had been examined and surveyed. The IBC "eliminated" these in several meetings held between 1910 and 1912, and all were grouped as the second series in the latter year.

With elimination of the second series, no further banco work of importance was performed for more than a decade. The IBC itself, in fact, had already slipped into a decade of inactivity. In 1911 it had been enlarged temporarily into an arbitration commission to attempt a solution of the nagging Chamizal dispute. The award had pleased neither nation and had been rejected by the United States. In 1911 too, the long reign of President Porfirio Díaz ended in revolution, and Mexico fell into a period of political ferment and strained relations with the United States that lasted until 1923. In 1914, finally, the able commissioners Mills and Puga were removed by their respective governments, Mills to be replaced, as he said, by "a discarded member of Congress, the bare mention of whose name to his former colleagues proved 'a source of merriment.'" All these influences bore hard on the IBC and converted it, when it could be said to exist at all, into a virtually dormant organization.

But its formative years had been fruitful. Summing up, General Mills wrote: "During the sixteen years of our active service . . . the Commission tried over one hundred cases of all kinds, disagreeing only in the Chamizal case, and preserved the peace and quiet of the entire Rio Grande border for these long years to the satisfaction of both governments and the people of the two nations." This record provided the basis for renewed progress once the United States and Mexico again began to speak civilly to each other.

The IBC came to life in 1922 with the appointment as United States commissioner of the colorful George Curry, former frontier lawman,

Opposite: *International Boundary Commission survey map for El Chamizal case Number 4.*

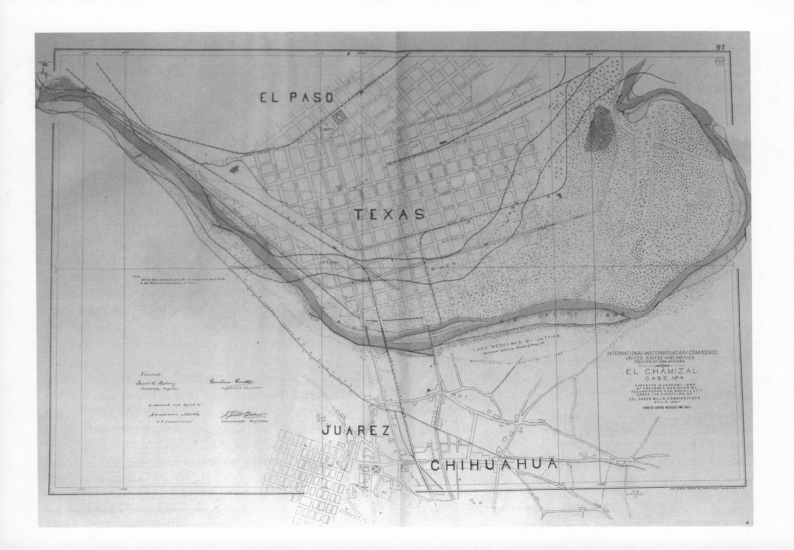

EL PASO

TEXAS

JUAREZ

CHIHUAHUA

INTERNATIONAL WATER BOUNDARY COMMISSION
UNITED STATES AND MEXICO
TREATIES OF 1884 AND 1889

EL CHAMIZAL
CASE Nº4

Rough Rider, and territorial governor of New Mexico. The following year Mexico named Gustavo P. Serrano as commissioner.

Banco surveys resumed at once, and by 1940 the banco problem had been brought largely under control. In sum, the Treaty of 1905 and the IBC by 1940 had eliminated 172 bancos, 107 of which, totaling 15,906 acres, passed to the United States and 65, totaling 8,075 acres, to Mexico. Two of these were on the Colorado River below Yuma, the rest on the Rio Grande. The disparity in favor of the United States reflected the denser population on the American side of the boundary and the consequent tendency of bancos there to be brought before the commission without delay.

Beginning in the 1930s, the IBC devoted less attention to banco work. Although another forty-three were eliminated between 1940 and 1963, the inauguration of extensive flood control and water apportionment programs turned the IBC into new and more important fields of activity that, as an incidental effect, promised to slow and in places halt the process of banco formation and thus to reduce the banco problem to minor proportions.

Water Apportionment, River Rectification, and Flood Control

Bancos were only one of several river problems whose magnitude, complexity, and urgency increased as the population along the water frontier increased in the opening decades of the twentieth century. For one, the floods that periodically ravaged the lower valleys of the Rio Grande and the Colorado now exacted a frightful toll in habitations, farm improvements, and crops. For another, with more and more people depending on the undependable flow of the boundary streams for irrigation water, the demand sometimes threatened to exceed the supply. How could the destructive force of the floods be minimized? How should the water supply be fairly divided between Mexicans and Americans? How might the flow be so controlled as to afford maximum benefit from what the streams could offer?

These were vital questions to the people who lived on the rivers and hence to the governments in Washington and Mexico City. So vital were they, in fact, that negotiations to find answers repeatedly collapsed under the weight of conflicting national interests. Not until the problems became so pressing as to admit no further delay did the United States and Mexico join forces for an earnest assault on them.

Early efforts to find a formula for equitable distribution centered on the El Paso-Juárez Valley. In dry years not enough water reached the valley for people on both sides of the river. And the expanding population of El Paso in the last decades of the nineteenth century, coupled with extensive irrigation developments underway upstream in the Mesilla Valley, forecast still worse times ahead. Diplomacy developed cogent arguments on both sides but no solution.

In 1888 the city of El Paso called in Colonel Anson Mills, not yet heading the American section of the IBC, to study the problem and recommend a solution. Mills proposed the construction of an international dam in the Pass of the North above town. This would impound the river and conserve water for use below in times of drought. The idea took hold and was later, after formation of the IBC with Mills as United States commissioner, vigorously championed in many quarters.

But a British firm had already begun work on a dam farther upstream, at Engle, New Mexico.

The river, with only one major tributary between El Paso and its source, could not supply water to two dams. A long contest ensued between proponents of the two sites. The British were at length eliminated from the dispute. And in 1905 the United States Congress, assured that the upstream dam would serve New Mexican as well as El Paso-Juárez needs, authorized construction of Elephant Butte Dam as a federal project.

This action cleared the way for an accord designed to assure a fair division of water between Mexican and American inhabitants of the El Paso-Juárez Valley. The Treaty of 1906 provided that, after completion of the Elephant Butte Dam, Mexico could receive sixty thousand acre-feet of water each year at the headgate of the old Spanish acequia above Juárez. This amount would be deemed sufficient for all needs on the Mexican side of the valley, and residents on the American side would be entitled to all remaining water in the river as far south as Fort Quitman, the lower limit of the valley. This arrangement took effect on completion of Elephant Butte Dam in 1915 and has generally worked to the satisfaction of both parties ever since.

Elephant Butte Dam on the Rio Grande, completed in 1915.

In 1933 Mexico and the United States took another large stride toward the elimination of frontier irritants in the El Paso-Juárez Valley. Under Commissioners Curry (1922–27) and Serrano (1923–31), the IBC conducted detailed engineering studies of the means by which the river channel might be rectified in the valley from El Paso downstream to Fort Quitman. Their successors, L. M. Lawson and Armando Santacruz, brought the project to fruition. In the Treaty of 1933 the two nations agreed to a joint program of straightening the river in this stretch of the valley, thereby preventing floods and stabilizing the boundary. The IBC was to direct the project and administer and maintain the works. As the United States expected to gain the greater benefit, it agreed to bear 88 percent of the cost while Mexico would pick up the bill for the remaining 12 percent.

Canalization work commenced in 1934 and ended in 1938. The project converted a channel of 155 miles length to one of 88 miles and involved the exchange of territory between the United States and Mexico of 5,121 acres, including right-of-way and tracts bounded by eliminated loops of the river. Of the latter, 175 were created by the rectification; 66 fell to the United States, 85 to Mexico, and 24 required no change of dominion, but neither country lost any territory not offset by gains. The cost totaled about $4 million.

Bordered by floodways and imprisoned by levees, the rectified river no longer posed much danger of flood to the El Paso-Juárez Valley, and the difficulties springing from an uncertain boundary line were obviated altogether. A similar project, carried on concurrently by the United States as a responsibility of the American section of the IBC, straightened and stabilized the river in the Mesilla Valley above El Paso and imparted even greater effectiveness to the international works below the twin cities.

The Colorado River and the lower Rio Grande yielded agreement less readily. Although only twenty miles in length, the international segment of the Colorado produced a disproportionate share of boundary problems. The need for an accord covering flood control and fair apportionment burst forth dramatically in 1905.

For some years the diversion of the Colorado through an American-built canal on Mexican soil into California's Imperial Valley had worried Mexicans dependent on its flow. In 1905 their worst fears were realized when the silting of canal intakes finally led the river to surmount its banks and cut a new channel through the Imperial Valley to the Salton Sea. For more than a year, the river emptied into the Salton Sea rather than the Gulf of California, and only massive aid from the Southern Pacific Railroad and the federal government enabled the private irrigation firm to restore the stream to its historic bed.

A special international commission was organized in 1908 to study the Colorado question, and in 1912 negotiations commenced looking to the formation of yet another commission with powers similar to or even greater than those of the IBC. But the bad relations that set in between the two nations at this time halted the talks. Meanwhile, attracted by the possibilities of irrigated farming widely publicized by the 1905 disaster, more and more people flocked to the Colorado lowlands to make the problem even worse, while upriver a burgeoning controversy among the states dependent on the Colorado added domestic complications to the international issue. When friendly relations between the United States and Mexico were finally restored in 1923, the Colorado was an item high on the diplomatic agenda.

Only slightly less pressing were issues on the lower Rio Grande. The same commission that in 1908 undertook studies of the Colorado also gave some attention to the lower Rio Grande. But all efforts at a solution broke over the rocklike stand of the Mexican representative, Beltrán y Puga, who also headed the Mexican section of the IBC, that Mexico "should have all the water she needs before the United States gets one drop."

His argument did not lack logic. Between Fort Quitman and the mouth of the Conchos, the

Rio Grande was not much of a river and indeed frequently ran dry. Below the Conchos, 70 percent of the water in the Rio Grande came from streams rising in Mexico, mainly the Conchos. The Pecos, Devils, and lesser American tributaries furnished the rest. Yet by the 1920s, such had been the agricultural growth of the lower valley, American users accounted for seventy percent of the water drawn for irrigation purposes. With the continued expansion of this population, agreement on fair division of the river waters took on increasing urgency.

The State Department did not believe that the IBC could handle the matter without another treaty, and in 1924 Congress authorized a joint commission to explore the possibilities. Mexico refused to cooperate unless the commission investigated the Colorado too. In 1928, therefore, the two nations formed the International Water Commission, composed of three representatives of each government, to study the lower Rio Grande, the Colorado, and even the little Tijuana on the coastal end of the California boundary. The commission collected a huge amount of data but could not reach agreements on which a treaty might be founded. In 1932 the commission was dissolved and its functions transferred to the IBC, which continued throughout the 1930s to gather data and search for solutions.

The deliberations developed many technical and legal arguments on both sides, but they resolved into one central issue: Mexico insisted on more water than the United States would concede. While investigations and negotiations dragged on, moreover, both nations proceeded with works that lay within their own territory but that, by affecting the behavior of the boundary streams, heightened the urgency for an accord. The United States undertook the Boulder Canyon project on the Colorado, the All-American Canal to the Imperial Valley, and works along the lower Rio Grande. Mexico constructed dams and reservoirs on the Rios Conchos, Salado, and San Juan. These developments, coupled with continued growth of population in the boundary valleys, finally brought the United States and Mexico to reconcile their divergent views and agree on a cooperative effort.

The details were set forth in a water treaty signed in Washington on February 3, 1944, and in an annexed minute of the IBC incorporating the results of exhaustive engineering and cost studies. The heart of the treaty lay in the agreement to construct, as a joint venture, three international storage dams for flood control and water conservation on the Rio Grande between the mouth of the Conchos and the Gulf of Mexico. The amount of water to be delivered to users on each side was specified in detail. The cost of construction, operation, and maintenance was to be prorated between the two countries in proportion to the amount of water each received. From the Colorado, Mexico was guaranteed an annual share of 1,500,000 acre-feet, 500,000 of which could be delivered at Mexico's option through the All-American Canal to a connecting canal dug on the other side of the boundary. Finally, the treaty transformed the IBC into the International Boundary and Water Commission (IBWC) and clothed it with new powers and responsibilities, mainly to plan, supervise construction, operate, and maintain the international dams and such hydroelectric power and additional flood control works as might prove desirable.

Construction began immediately on the first of the three dams. The Falcón Dam, twenty miles upstream from Rio Grande City and Camargo, was completed and put into operation in 1953.

With associated power plants, it cost $46 million, the United States bearing 58.6 percent of the cost of the dam and half the cost of the power plant. Providing a storage capacity of more than 4,500,000 acre-feet, Falcón Dam watered 750,000 acres of American farmland and 500,000 acres of Mexican farmland. It cost the United States about $26 million but within a decade had saved the United States more than $100 million in flood damages. At the dedication of the work on October 19, 1953, President Dwight Eisenhower summed up its meaning: "More than a mute monument to the ingenuity of engineers, this Falcón Dam is living testimony to the understanding and cooperation binding our two peoples."

With completion of Falcón Dam, the IBWC undertook surveys to determine the best place for the second dam authorized by the Water Treaty of 1944. The Amistad site just below the mouth of Devils River, twelve miles above Del Rio and Ciudad Acuña, proved most advantageous, and construction of Amistad Dam began in 1963. Presidents Nixon and Diaz Ordaz inaugurated the completed dam on September 8, 1969. This Friendship dam created a lake covering 65,000 acres, 32,000 feet long and 254 feet above the former river bed, with a storage capacity of 5,535,000 acre feet. The U.S. share of the construction costs was $72.3 million for the dam and $31 million for the power plant.

The third dam provided for in the treaty of 1944 remains in the future.

For a century the boundary rivers thrust on the United States and Mexico a wide range of complex and portentous problems that contributed chronically to international discord. The Treaties of 1884, 1889, 1905, 1906, 1933, and 1944 laid the foundation for resolving them all.

They were solid diplomatic achievements, as were the implementing activities of the personnel of the boundary commission. Although overshadowed by the more spectacular Indian, filibuster, revolutionary, and bandit violence, and thus largely unnoticed by the citizens of the two nations, the spirit of international cooperation represented by these accords established a trend that culminated in 1963 with the settlement, by the Chamizal treaty, of the last important boundary controversy.

Chamizal

5

ONE BOUNDARY PROBLEM THE OLD IBC COULD NEVER MASTER—
Chamizal. A small tract of about six hundred acres bordering
the Rio Grande between El Paso and Juárez, it gained its name
from a characteristic brushy thicket that once grew there.
Although not a banco in shape, Chamizal resembled one in size
and in its character as a parcel of land that had migrated from
one side of the river to the other. Yet it took on a significance
far exceeding that of any banco and out of all proportion to its
intrinsic value.

Part of the explanation lay in its urban location; the stakes
here were higher than in most banco situations. Part lay in confusion over the exact process of river action by which the tract

had been formed and consequently over how to apply the treaty provisions governing national ownership and jurisdiction. And finally, the explanation lay in national pride; continued disagreement charged the issue with an emotion that in turn hardened the disagreement still more.

For nearly seventy years, Chamizal persisted as a source of contention and irritation. After the conclusion of the 1944 Water Treaty, it remained the only serious boundary controversy between Mexico and the United States, and its settlement in 1963 represented a diplomatic success important primarily for its positive effect on Mexican-American relations in general and secondarily for the local benefits it produced.

The Problem

Before the river stabilization programs of the twentieth century, the El Paso-Juárez Valley was a notoriously unstable segment of the river boundary. Winding back and forth on its floodplain, the Rio Grande carved out bancos and "islands" by the score. Most vulnerable was the extreme upper end of the valley, where the river debouched from its rockbound channel through the Pass of the North and in a sweeping arc changed direction from south to southeast. The current in this bend ate away the southern bank and built up the northern. Here the Spanish El Paso del Norte (later Juárez) rose on the right bank in the seventeenth century, and here the American El Paso rose on the left bank in the middle of the nineteenth century.

The shifting course of the Rio Grande was no more than an inconvenience to José Ponce de León when he received El Chamizal as part of a land grant from the Mexican government in 1827, for both sides of the river belonged to Mexico. The trouble came when the United States took over the north side pursuant to the Treaty of Guadalupe Hidalgo. By the time Emory and Salazar fixed the boundary here in 1852, the river had moved to the south of its 1827 channel by about half a mile. By 1895 it had cut still farther southward from one-fourth to a full mile.

Pedro Ignacio García, who inherited El Chamizal from his grandfather in 1866, nursed a serious grievance. Because of the river's movement, his land now lay on the Texas side of the river, and he had "not dared to occupy my aforesaid land, fearful, as I was . . . that some personal injury might befall me from the part of a few North Americans, who supposing this land to belong to the United States of North America, pretended to come into possession of the same." On García's behalf, Mexico brought the case before the IBC on November 4, 1895.

The case appeared simple. If the river had changed its course slowly and gradually, the boundary had moved with it and Chamizal belonged to the United States. If the change had occurred suddenly—avulsively—then Chamizal still belonged to Mexico, and the boundary remained in the old channel surveyed by Emory and Salazar in 1852. The task for the IBC was to decide which process had caused the change and, in keeping with the Treaty of 1884, to define the boundary accordingly.

The testimony of old settlers and the investigations of IBC engineers showed that the change in the river channel could not be definitively ascribed to either erosion or avulsion but rather to a process that fell somewhere between the two extremes. The evidence disclosed that before 1864 the channel had moved southward slowly and gradually. After 1864, however, it had progressed at a greatly accelerated pace that, while not a sudden or avulsive move from one channel to another, nevertheless was perceptible and at times violent.

That the Chamizal had been formed in this manner Commissioners Mills and Osorno agreed. The disagreement centered on how to apply the Treaty of 1884 to a situation in which the river action could not be labeled wholly and clearly one of the two processes described by the treaty.

The Mexican commissioner argued that "Any change other than *slow* and *gradual* does not alter the boundary line." Everyone agreed that between 1852 and 1864 the change had indeed been slow and gradual but that after 1864 it had not been slow and gradual. Therefore, concluded Osorno, the boundary remained as established by Emory and Salazar in 1852, and Chamizal was Mexican territory.

Not so, countered the American commissioner. Erosion may be violent and perceptible as well as slow and gradual. Clearly the river had not abandoned the old channel and cut a new one; it had simply moved, at times more rapidly than at others, by a process of eroding soil from the south bank and depositing it on the north. Therefore, as set forth in the treaty, the boundary had moved with the river and Chamizal was American territory.

The dispute thus focused on differing interpretations of the pertinent treaty provisions—that the boundary moved with the river if the river moved as a result of "natural causes through the slow and gradual erosion and deposit of alluvium and not by the abandonment of an existing river bed and the opening of a new one." Logically, this language could admit either the Mills or the Osorno interpretation.

This being true, to Mexico the question now seemed to call for a new approach. In 1898 her Foreign Secretary suggested that it be submitted to the head of a third power for arbitration. To Washington, however, the case was not one for "friendly compromise" but for application of established rules to a specific situation. Perhaps by naming a third commissioner, either Mexican or American, to sit temporarily with the IBC the established rules might be made to work. Mexico saw no hope in this formula, and there the matter rested for a decade.

During this time another boundary matter arose to complicate the Chamizal question.

Droughts in 1895 and 1896 left the Rio Grande at El Paso-Juárez dry or nearly dry for several months at a time in both years, and large deposits of sand accumulated to obstruct the channel. Too, the river just below El Paso lengthened its course through erosion and thereby greatly decreased the gradient of the bed. In May 1897 a great flood poured down the river and, encountering these adverse conditions, spread over much of the two cities.

IBC engineering studies revealed that repetition of such a disaster might be prevented by an artificial cut across the neck of a river loop that, intruding on Chamizal on the east, jutted northward into El Paso. The United States and Mexican governments approved the proposal, Mexico with the understanding that the boundary would remain in the abandoned bed, that she would retain jurisdiction over the enclave thus thrown into Texas, and that her position in the Chamizal dispute would in no way be prejudiced. As an intercity project, the cut was completed in April 1899, and in 1907 the IBC placed boundary monuments in the old river bed.

In this manner, Córdova "Island," a tract of nearly four hundred acres of Mexican domain, came to rest on the American side of the river. With title to Chamizal clouded and Córdova projecting incongruously into El Paso, the orderly development of both cities was hampered and all the troubles of a vague boundary, magnified by the urban context, thrust on Mexican and American authorities.

In 1907, on Mexican initiative, the two governments resumed the attempt to find a formula for resolving the Chamizal issue. The Mexican ambassador in Washington suggested the formation of a special arbitration commission consisting of the two commissioners of the IBC and a Canadian jurist. Although diplomats debated a number of plans in the next three years, in the end they came back to the Mexican idea.

By a convention signed on June 24, 1910, Mexico and the United States agreed to enlarge the IBC by the addition of a Canadian member and to empower it as an arbitration commission. The Canadian was to serve as chairman and exercise the same vote as the American and Mexican representatives. Either by unanimous or majority vote, the commission was to decide which nation, under the Treaty of 1884, possessed title to El Chamizal, and for both governments the decision was to be final and conclusive. With the aid of Canada, Mexico and the United States squared away for another major effort at settling this long-standing source of international discord.

The Arbitration of 1911

The arbitration commission convened in El Paso on May 15, 1911. Eugene Lafleur, former professor of international law at McGill University, was the Canadian jurist and as specified by the 1910 convention served as presiding commissioner. The other two members were the U.S. boundary commissioner Anson Mills and the Mexican commissioner Fernando Beltrán y Puga. The commission reduced the problem to six questions on which the parties to the dispute, through legal "agents," presented arguments and counterarguments and on which the three commissioners then voted.

The first question found Mexico advancing a proposition that ignored the entire history of the boundary. "Was the boundary line established by the Treaties of 1848 and 1853 along the Rio Grande a fixed and invariable line?" Yes, ran the Mexican argument; it was surveyed on the ground and laid down on the map, and the language of the treaties contemplated that it remain there regardless of changes in the river. Lafleur and Mills both pointed out, however, that everything the two governments had ever said and done concerning the boundary, especially their negotiation of the Treaties of 1884, 1889, and 1905, contradicted the Mexican assertion, and so too did all the principles and practices of the international law of boundary streams. By a vote of two to one, the commission rejected the Mexican theory of the fixed and invariable line.

The second question proved the only one of which the commissioners could unite: "Has the United States acquired title to the Chamizal tract by prescription?"—by reason, that is, of "undisturbed, uninterrupted, and unchallenged possession" for half a century. The evidence clearly showed that possession had hardly gone unchallenged by Mexico. It revealed too the absence of an ingredient vital to the prescription theory— that possession be peaceable. Any Mexican who attempted to occupy Chamizal risked a violent reaction from American citizens. The fact was well known and had discouraged all such attempts. All three commissioners voted to throw out the prescription argument.

Mexico also hoped to win the case through a negative answer to the third question: "Does the Treaty of 1884 apply to all changes in the river subsequent to the survey of 1852?" The Mexican agent declared that the Treaty of 1884 was not retroactive, that it applied only to river changes that occurred after 1884, and that therefore it could not govern the disposition of El Chamizal. Mills and Lafleur had no difficulty meeting this contention. First, practically all the important changes in the Rio Grande had taken place before 1884, and to assume that the treaty had no relevance to them was to credit its negotiators with engaging in a meaningless exercise. International law did not admit interpretations that rendered a treaty provision meaningless; it must be supposed that a treaty was intended to accomplish something. Second, the Treaty of 1884 had been consistently applied retroactively with no objection from Mexico until now. Lafleur and Mills voted yes, Puga no. The Treaty of 1884 applied to the Chamizal case.

The fourth question rolled out the rock on which the deliberations of 1896–97 had shattered. "Was the whole of the Chamizal tract . . . formed by slow and gradual erosion and deposit of alluvium within the meaning of Article I of the Convention of 1884?" Neither party to the dispute came up with any new arguments. Mexico answered no; part had been formed by rapid erosion. The United States answered yes. The treaty provided for only two kinds of river action, erosion and avulsion, asserted Mills. Chamizal had obviously not been cut by avulsion. Therefore it had to have been erosion—even though faster at some times than at others. On this question the presiding commissioner joined with the Mexican commissioner to vote no. The treaty, he said, clearly qualified the kind of erosion meant as "slow and gradual," and the evidence showed that part of the tract had not been formed by slow and gradual erosion.

The fifth and sixth questions flowed logically from the fourth. "Was the formation of the Chamizal tract up to 1864 due to slow and gradual erosion and deposit of alluvium within the meaning of the Treaty of 1884?" "Was the whole erosion which occurred in 1864 and after that date slow and gradual within the meaning of the Treaty of 1884?" Given the evidence, the questions dictated the answers. On the fifth Lafleur and Puga voted yes. On the sixth they voted no so far as the period of 1864–68 was concerned. In their view, changes after 1868, which remained undocumented, could have no bearing on the question, for if the river quit moving by slow and gradual erosion in 1864, then the boundary quit moving with the river in 1864.

Mills perceived the drift of this reasoning. The majority answers to the fifth and sixth questions pointed to a division of the Chamizal tract along the line of the 1864 channel. Refusing to vote on either question, he maintained that the commission had departed from the terms of the convention creating it and also from the Treaty of 1884. The former empowered the commissioners to award Chamizal to one of the two contestants but said nothing about splitting it between them. The latter defined only two kinds of river action, erosion and avulsion, that affected the location of the boundary; the commission had invented a third, rapid or violent erosion, and made it the decisive factor in the case. And finally, Mills contended that as a practical matter the 1864 channel could not be traced on the ground, and such a solution would therefore prove unworkable.

Based on the vote on the six questions, however, this was the arbitration award announced by the presiding commissioner on June 15, 1911. Title to that part of Chamizal lying between the 1852 and the 1864 channels remained with the United States, and title to the rest passed to Mexico. The problem of finding the 1864 channel was not a matter of law, Lafleur reasoned, but of engineering, and the award decision did not touch on that aspect of the solution.

"The difference between tweedledum and tweedledee was never before so accurately defined in diplomacy," editorialized the *New York World*. "By crossing a street or turning a corner, citizens of El Paso will find themselves under the dominion of another nation and what that will mean in the matter of conflict of laws and encouragement of license may be readily understood. A comic-opera librettist never created a more diverting situation."

Neither Mexico nor the United States was satisfied with the award, and the commissioners of both filed dissenting opinions. Mexico, however, brought herself to accept the decision. The United States did not.

International law afforded ample precedent for rejecting an arbitral award that departed from the terms of the controlling convention, in this case the Convention of June 24, 1910. In the view of Commissioner Mills, this document required an award of Chamizal either to the United States or Mexico. It did not permit an award dividing it. The State Department accepted Mills's reasoning, and on August 24, 1911, the United States formally rejected the arbitral award.

A second major attempt at settlement had failed, and the failure, under circumstances that could be seen as American bad faith, aggravated an already serious controversy. However, as Professor Charles Timm, the leading authority on boundary history, has pointed out, "the very failure of the arbitration is a patent indication that the nature of the Chamizal matter was not of a sort to lend itself to settlement by that method." Contending that it was instead a matter for conventional diplomacy, he wrote in 1940:

> The non-arbitral nature of El Chamizal was touched upon obliquely by William Cullen Dennis, agent for the United States, during the conduct of the case. As he pointed out, the parties had an unequal stake in the question and furthermore, to find for Mexico would mean the creation of many problems rather than the solution of one. It was perhaps fortunate for the United States that the final award has opened a way by which the United States might escape the consequences of error in judgment, if it may be so called, that allowed the matter to go to arbitration in the first place.

Fruitless Negotiation, 1911–62

Efforts to find a solution continued intermittently for nearly half a century after the 1911 arbitration. Surprisingly, despite considerable Mexican bitterness over the American rejection of the award, negotiations that took place in conventional diplomatic channels between 1911 and 1913 made progress. Most of the proposals discussed at this time contemplated exchanges of territory linking Chamizal with such other trouble spots as San Elizario Island, El Horcón Banco, and Morteritos Island. Negotiations collapsed, however, in the wake of American refusal to recognize the regime of Victoriano Huerta.

Not until the early 1930s was there cause for renewed optimism. In 1930 the IBC drew up the plan for river rectification in the El Paso-Juárez Valley that formed the basis for the Treaty of 1933. This plan called for straightening the river in the entire length of the valley from the Pass of the North to Fort Quitman. The rectified channel would be carried across or around both the Chamizal and Córdova tracts. Here was an opportunity to stabilize the boundary between El Paso and Juárez, to treat Córdova together with all the other exchanges of territory the rectification program entailed, and to settle on some formula for routing the river in relation to Chamizal.

In negotiations in Mexico City in 1932, the Mexican Foreign Secretary linked the proposed

President John F. Kennedy, who pushed the treaty to a conclusion.

rectification program with an earlier State Department plan involving the Pious Fund. This was a substantial fund of money set up by Spain and the Catholic Church in 1697 for the support of Jesuit missions in California. The United States claimed it when California became American territory under the Treaty of Guadalupe Hidalgo in 1848. In 1902 the Permanent Court of Arbitration at the Hague, to which the claim had been submitted for arbitration, judged Mexico liable to the United States for an initial payment of nearly $1½ million and subsequent annual payments in perpetuity of $43,050. No payments had been made since 1914. The United States at one time had offered to cancel this obligation in return for clear title to Chamizal. In a treaty combining such an exchange with the agreement on river rectification, the American ambassador and Mexican Foreign Secretary believed they at last had hit on a workable formula. What happened to dash this hope is not apparent, but the Treaty of 1933 stipulated that river rectification work would begin below the Chamizal and Córdova tracts rather than above as proposed by the IBC.

Meanwhile, with the continued growth of El Paso and Juárez, the problems posed by clouded title to Chamizal and the existence of Mexican Córdova Island in the midst of American El Paso grew yearly more serious. With the passage of time, the problems could be expected to become steadily more serious and the prospects of settlement steadily less likely. Such a settlement could come only through rational compromise and, given the complexity, confusion, and emotion that the issue had accumulated in its sixty-seven-year history, only through the intervention of the chief executives of the two nations. Perceiving these truths, Presidents John F. Kennedy and López Mateos moved in 1962 to break the deadlock.

Signing ceremony with Ambassador Thomas C. Mann and Foreign Minister Manuel Tello.

The Treaty of 1963

The initiative came from the Mexican president and met a cordial response from the American president. On June 30, 1962, they issued a joint communique declaring that the State Department and the Ministry of Foreign Relations had been instructed to work together toward a complete solution of the problem. As President Kennedy believed that the United States had acted unwisely and unjustly in rejecting the 1911 arbitral award, the central task for the diplomats was no longer to reconcile divergent views but simply to update the 1911 award and fit it to modern conditions. Without prejudice to the juridical bases of their previous positions, both governments sought a practical and just solution. Cooperating closely with the IBWC, the diplomats came up with such a solution, which was incorporated into a memorandum submitted to the two presidents on July 17, 1963. Approved by them, the memorandum was then reworked into a treaty signed in Mexico City on August 29, 1963, by Ambassador Thomas C. Mann and Foreign Minister Manuel Tello.

The solution agreed to in the treaty promised Mexico substantially what it had been awarded by the arbitration commission in 1911—a boundary along the approximate course of the river in 1864. But the 1963 solution avoided the chief practical drawback of the 1911 solution. Instead of tracing an invisible boundary line through the heart of El Paso, the Rio Grande was to be moved back to a course close to its 1864 location and, confined in a concrete channel, constituted as an easily recognized boundary. The exact route of the relocated river was determined in such manner as to eliminate the troublesome Córdova Island enclave and to cut to Juárez 437 acres of El Paso, the amount

both governments agreed that Mexico would have gained by the 1911 award.

Thus from Mexico the United States would receive the northern half of Córdova Island, 193 acres. Between the relocated river and the existing channel, Juárez would absorb 366 acres west of the remaining half of Córdova Island and 264 acres east of it, for a total of 630 acres. This figure represented the original 437-acre claim and an additional 193 acres as compensation for the part of Córdova Island Mexico would yield to the United States.

The treaty also defined procedures for the transfer of the 630 acres to Mexico. The United States agreed to pass title to Mexico unencumbered. Mexico would then convey title to a private Mexican bank. The bank in turn would pay the Mexican government the estimated value of the structures and other improvements on it. As there were no structures anywhere on Córdova Island, no monetary complication arose there.

For the tracts formerly under United States jurisdiction, however, the task would be formidable. Before title could be conveyed to Mexico, the U.S. government would have to buy out American property owners and move about 5,500 people elsewhere. In addition, it would have to provide them with housing, schools, and other public facilities. Then, in accordance with the treaty, it would join with Mexico, each bearing half the cost, to relocate the river in its new channel and to construct new international bridges. Finally, it would erect new border control facilities to replace those passing to Mexico. Most of the responsibility for carrying out this program fell to the IBWC, which also had the task of coordinating the efforts of city, state, and federal agencies. The program was estimated to cost $50 million.

Although the United States yielded almost entirely to the historic Mexican contention, the Chamizal settlement was widely regarded as well worth the price. Forecasting the conclusion of the treaty, on July 18, 1963, President Kennedy declared that the solution "will make a significant contribution to relations between the United States and Mexico and will contribute to the welfare and orderly development of El Paso, Texas, and Ciudad Juárez, Chihuahua."

Aerial view of the area affected by rechannelling the Rio Grande between El Paso and Ciudad Juárez.

Execution of the treaty would bear out President Kennedy's optimistic prediction.

The Chamizal treaty erased the last border dispute of consequence in the eventful history of the international boundary. The Mexican-American War began in a boundary dispute, and the

Gadsden Treaty flowed from another. In the former the United States prevailed by violence, in
the latter by the implied threat of violence.
Thereafter, every boundary dispute and every
boundary problem was settled by peaceful
means. With Chamizal out of the way, with the
major border improvement works that have been
put in place in the twentieth century, and with
well-established machinery for handling every
form of border problem, it seemed unlikely that
a dispute like Chamizal could ever again trouble
the border.   The Treaty of 1963 thus stands as
a significant landmark in the history of Mexican-
American relations, and the works that have
taken shape according to its provisions stand as
a monument to the mature spirit of friendship
and cooperation in which two peoples face each
other across the international boundary, United
States and Mexico.

*Presidents Adolofo López Mateos and Lyndon B.
Johnson meet at the finally setted border in September
1964.*

Suggested Readings

BARTLETT, JOHN R. *Personal Narrative of Explorations and Incidents in Texas, New Mexico, California, Sonora and Chihuahua, Connected with the United States and Mexican Boundary Commission during the Years, 1850, '51, '52, and '53.* 2 vols., New York, 1954.

CASTILLO, RICHARD GRISWOLD del. *The Treaty of Guadalupe Hidalgo: A Legacy of Conflict.* Norman, Okla., 1990.

EMORY, WILLIAM H. *Report on the United States and Mexican Boundary Survey* . . . by William H. Emory. 3 vols., Washington, D.C., 1857.

GARBER, PAUL N. *The Gadsden Treaty.* Philadelphia, 1923.

GOETZMANN, WILLIAM H. *Army Exploration in the American West, 1803–1863.* New Haven, Conn., 1959.

GOETZMANN, WILLIAM H. *Exploration and Empire: The Explorer and the Scientist in the Winning of the American West.* New York, 1966.

GREGG, R. D. *The Influence of Border Troubles on Relations between the United States and Mexico, 1876–1910.* Baltimore, 1937.

LISS, SHELDON B. *A Century of Disagreement: The Chamizal Conflict 1864–1964.* Washington, D.C., 1965.

MARTINEZ, OSCAR J. *Troublesome Border.* Tucson, Ariz., 1988.

MERK, FREDERICK. *Manifest Destiny and Mission in American History.* New York, 1963.

METZ, LEON C. *Border: The U.S.-Mexico Line.* Mangan Books, El Paso, Tex. 1989.

RIPPY, J. FRED. *The United States and Mexico.* New York, 1926.

RITTENHOUSE, JACK D. *The Story of Disturnell's Treaty Map.* Santa Fe, N.M., 1965.

TIMM, CHARLES A. *The International Boundary Commission, United States and Mexico.* Austin, Tex., 1941.

WALLACE, EDWARD S. *The Great Reconnaissance: Soldiers, Artists and Scientists on the Frontier, 1848–1861.* Boston and Toronto, 1955.

WEINBERG, ALBERT K. *Manifest Destiny: A Study of Nationalist Expansionism in American History.* Chicago, 1963.

WHEAT, CARL I. *Mapping the Transmississippi West, 1540–1861.* 5 vols., San Francisco, 1957–63.

The Chamizal Since 1963

by Franklin G. Smith, Superintendent, Chamizal National Memorial, 1967–1991

EPILOGUE

International Compliance

On January l6, l964, President Lyndon B. Johnson, on behalf of the United States, proclaimed the ratification of the Chamizal Convention placing the terms of the pact in force as of January l4.[1] The nations had agreed on land exchange, river control work, and equal cost sharing for the channel changes, two railroad bridges and three pedestrian and vehicular bridges. The International Boundary and Water Commission was assigned the responsibility for implementing the agreement. Now diplomatic success had to be turned into physical change in the center of the two cities making up the hemisphere's largest border community.

While the United States had agreed to the Convention, separate specific legislation was required to authorize the actions and to appropriate funds. The administration introduced the authorization bill prepared by the Department of State (and IBWC). Both houses of Congress acted quickly, and on April 29, 1964, Public Law 88-300 was signed as an ". . . Act to facilitate compliance with the Convention between the United States of America and the United Mexican States signed on August 29, 1963." It authorized the appropriation of $44.9 million for the purposes of the law. Legislation to appropriate the necessary money was included in the budget for the Department of State, and Public Law 88-527, including $30 million for the first Chamizal work, was signed August 31, 1964.

In the meantime, IBWC Commissioners Joseph F. Friedkin (United States) and David Herrera Jordán (Mexico) assembled their teams of specialists. Land acquisition was clearly the first priority, and the first United States purchase was contracted on December 10, 1964. Apart from the 630.38 acres to be transferred to Mexico, Friedkin's staff had to acquire 113.16 acres for the relocation of railroads, circulation routes, and public facilities. This entailed acquisition of 186 commercial and industrial buildings, 14 public buildings and other public facilities including school land and Public Service Board sewage treatment facilities. The largest problem came with the relocation of people. There were 596 single- and multiple-family dwellings and 65 tenements, home to about 5,500 individuals. Through agreement with the City of El Paso, which had voiced concerns during the hearing on P.L.88-300, properties were acquired at replacement costs, rather than appraised value,

and 1,158 claims for ancillary costs (including relocation allotments) were paid. This uprooting of families made headlines, but the IBWC displayed considerable empathy for those affected by the project and there was little public criticism of their actions.[2]

An additional task for the U.S. Section of the IBWC was to plan the use of the 193.8 acres of the northern portion of Cordova Island to be transferred from Mexico to the United States.

In the next four years, the two nations completed the relocation of 4.3 miles of river channel (concrete-lined and designed to retain the waters of the largest flood to be anticipated in a 500-year period), completed the five bridges and associated ports of entry, and on the U.S. side alone relocated 11.7 miles of railroad track and 1.74 miles of irrigation canals. Cost to the U.S. government was under $43.5 million; associated costs of highway construction, including the new Border Highway and connections with the new Interstate 10 would be more than $40 million. Apart from the inconveniences associated with any urban changes, the interference with border crossings—then about 30 million people per year—was negligible![3]

On October 28, 1967, Presidents Gustavo Díaz Ordaz and Lyndon Baines Johnson signed Final Minute 214 (specific stipulations) of the Convention, placing the land exchange into effect and initiating construction of the river's new channel. It was appropriate that the ceremony was held at the freshly completed commemorative structure of the Chamizal Park of Mexico under the profile of Benito Juárez and his words, "The law has always been my sword and my shield." Dignitaries from the United States entered Mexico through the old route, and returned across the new Bridge of the Americas through the new Port of Entry.

On December 13, 1968, the two presidents returned to open the new channel of the river, inaugurating the final river channel, and on January 18, 1969, the last construction work of the Convention was completed. Honoring their leadership through the project, commissioners Joseph F. Friedkin and David Herrera Jordán were advanced to the personal rank of ambassador.

One legal matter remained. The pre-Convention boundaries of Texas and the stated boundaries of the United States as of 1848 had not included the 193.8 acres of Cordova Island acquired under the Convention. Thus Texas laws and legal control did not extend to this land, which included the sites of the new Port of Entry, the new Bowie High School, a public housing project, circulation routes, and a proposed national monument and culture center. Technically, the Cordova Island tract transferred from Mexico was a federal enclave between Texas and Mexico! To correct the situation the Texas legislature formally requested that the land be added legally to the state, and H.R.8539, "giving the consent of Congress to the addition of land to the State of Texas..." was introduced by Congressman Richard C. White of El Paso, March 10, 1969, and passed into law by the 91st Congress.

The City of El Paso

A 1960 approach by community leaders of El Paso to presidential nominee John F. Kennedy was pragmatic, with idealistic overtones. Contacts across the border on a daily basis left no doubt about the feelings of Mexico, and indeed of Latin America, regarding the U.S. rejection of the 1911 Arbitration Commission findings. The service to the nation in finding an immediate and equitable solution was obvious.[4] At the same time, eliminating future arguments about the land between the 1852 and 1895 river channels would free much of the center of the city for future growth.

The city, county, and El Paso Independent School District were willing to contribute—within reason. The immediate tax loss to the city government alone would be $306,900 per year at 1964 assessed value. The IBWC agreed from the beginning to provide funds for replacement of facilities such as the Public Service Board sewage treatment plant, and the sum of $9.8 million was eventually set for partial replacement of the roads, utility systems, fourteen public buildings, and other public lands and improvements. The leaders of the community found this acceptable, although not lavish. Two cases are worth mentioning.[5]

First was the matter of the placement of the headquarters and the alien detention facility of the U.S. Border Patrol, which were then located on land to be transferred to Mexico. The only location possible for the IBWC, because of strict geographic limits on the United States land to be acquired under the Convention, was on part of the 193 acres of Cordova Island to be received from Mexico.

The *1964 City Planning Department Report* on the Chamizal stated:

> To avoid the necessity of relocating the [United States Border Patrol] detention facility on the land to be owned by the Federal Government on Cordova Island adjacent to the new international bridge and the proposed national monument park, the City of El Paso is donating to the Federal Government a twenty (20) acre site valued in excess of $200,000 for the Border Patrol Sector Headquarters and the Immigration and Naturalization Service Alien Detention Facility. It is the opinion of the people of El Paso that an alien detention facility adjacent to the new river channel and port of entry would be incompatible with the objectives of the Treaty and a National Park area.

The power behind this arrangement was Mayor Judson Williams, who gained the support of the City Council in the matter and built the agreement with the organizations concerned.

The land which had been originally intended for the facility was added to the acreage proposed for the national monument and culture center.

A second matter of note was Bowie High School, which served much of the Second Ward—the Segundo Barrio—including the entire Chamizal area and the central border portion of the city. For two generations "La Bowie" had been a symbol to students and alumni of achievement, both academic and athletic. Many Bowie graduates were the first in their families to earn diplomas and go on to college. (Alumni chapters of Bowie exist as far away as Los Angeles.) And now the campus of Bowie High School would be cut in two by the new river channel!

A new school was an obviously appropriate use for a part of the Cordova tract, and 60.8 acres were set aside. Funding was partly from a bond issue passed in 1967, combined with funds provided by the IBWC as compensation for the land and facilities taken. A modern design, in increments capable of future expansion, was planned to complement the style of the proposed national memorial.

The city also programmed $775,000 for urban renewal acquisitions, bringing its initial cash contribution to well over $2 million. Overall, the entire process had been a model of cooperation between all levels of government involved.[6]

Other concerns also led community leaders to appear at the House and Senate Hearings on both the implementation bill and the various appropriation bills and ask Congress to consider specific inclusions for four items of concern. The Department of State, through the IBWC, agreed.

The first two items could be handled through the Convention legislation (Public Law 88-300). One was a guarantee that the people displaced would receive satisfactory reimbursement for their property, plus moving expenses. The second was that the IBWC would assume the responsibility of relocation of the American Canal, part of which would be affected by the Convention. Both were in the IBWC plans, but gained force through the city's stance.

The third item was the construction of the Chamizal Memorial Highway to create a river route as part of the inner circle circulation of the city and county. This required separate legislation, drafted and introduced concurrently in the Senate by Senator Ralph Yarbrough (S. 2360) and in the House by Congressman Richard White (H.R. 11555) on October 12, 1963, and signed as Public Law 89-795 by President Johnson on November 8, 1966.

The fourth consideration was more complex. The city requested that a "national monument and culture center" be considered for development on part of the Cordova Island acquisition.[7]

Chamizal National Memorial

To maintain the high quality of the areas administered by the National Park Service, Department of the Interior, and to make sure that only those places with unique qualifications in history and natural science are included in the National Park System, the process of establishing such areas has been subject to a number of controls.[8] In early 1964 the IBWC informed the National Park Service of the possibility of a legislative proposal by the Department of State, and in October of that year the first meetings were held with the IBWC and city leaders in El Paso.

The National Park Service process began with an historical analysis; responsibility was assigned the Southwest Regional Office, in Santa Fe, New Mexico, and Robert M. Utley, then regional historian, prepared the work which forms the body of this book. His findings were clear. The proposed site carried national significance beyond the Chamizal Convention itself. The background history of the Chamizal, beginning with the explorations and geodesic achievements of the International Boundary Survey, 1849-57, was exemplary in the demonstration that people of widely different cultural and linguistic backgrounds can work together toward a common objective and in the process build understanding and friendship. The continuing work of the various boundary commissions, involving a series of treaties to resolve border problems, maintained this thread of cooperation even when the two nations were in opposition on other matters. Further, this attitude of coexistence characterized the continuing border interaction, where residents were joined by geography while divided by the international boundary. The unique event of the Chamizal Convention, involving a major land action and the peaceful withdrawal of both land claimed by the United States (the area between the 1852 and 1866 river courses) and land certainly owned by the United States (the eastern segment ceded to allow for the new river channel) offered a superb opportunity to tell the story in a central location.[9] The Secretary of the Interior's Advisory Board on National Parks, Historic Sites, Buildings, and Monuments agreed and so recommended to Secretary of the Interior Stewart Udall.

On April 13, 1965, Congressman Richard C. White introduced H.R. 7402, a ". . . bill to provide for the establishment of a Chamizal Treaty National Memorial in El Paso, Texas," and hearings began in the House and later the Senate. The discussions during these hearings defined the intent of the Congress regarding the development of the proposed memorial.

First, the word "treaty" was seen as cumbersome and too limiting in its subject matter and was dropped from the title: the memorial would tell the history of the border since 1848. This also was defined in the title of the proposed area: a "national memorial" commemorates historical events or persons beyond the geographical limits of the physical location, and as such Chamizal would be in the company of the Lincoln Memorial, Jefferson Memorial, and the Jefferson National Expansion Memorial in Saint Louis, Missouri, among others.

Second, the overall concept of the use of the Cordova Island tract was considered: the Secretary of the Interior was not to proceed until satisfied with the integrity of the surrounding environment. This was no problem. Secretary Udall approved the plans for the land use as commensurate with the memorial in 1967.

Third, the "culture center" concept would be defined, at least in part, through consultation with the city, the university, and other individuals and groups in El Paso. This involvement of the local citizens would prove beneficial as the planning continued.

On June 30, 1966, President Johnson signed Public Law 89-479. It authorized, but did not appropriate, $2,060,000 for the development of the memorial. Planning was then assigned to the Southwest Regional Office of the National Park Service and its Western Office of Design and Construction in San Francisco.

Planning for a park on the Mexican side had progressed rapidly under the guidance of Licenciado Francisco Ruiz Obregón, Presidente de la Junta Federal de Mejoras Materiales, Secretaría del Patrimonio Nacional for Chihuahua (Director of Public Works, Department of National Public Lands) with support by Don Luis Villalobos Rendón, Representante del Programa Nacional Fronterizo, in Ciudad Juárez (Representative for the National Frontier Development Program, or ProNaF, reporting to the ministry in charge of national parks.) The 764-acre park was planned as a major public-use area, centering around a commemorative structure suitable for public ceremonies. Plans included athletic fields, a tree farm, botanical garden, sculptures, and fountains. Eventually, under Ruiz Obregón's successor, Ingeniero Rafael Pérez-Serna, the park expanded with an indoor/outdoor archeological museum, plantings to display the flora of the entire border, a concession area and extensive children's playgrounds. Later additions added a world-class soccer stadium and the site for the annual Juárez Fair. These gentlemen and their staffs were entirely gracious and supportive of the National Park Service in the planning and construction phases of Chamizal National Memorial, as were many of the staff of other federal projects in Ciudad Juárez.

With only 55 acres to work with, National Park Service planners felt that the best route to complement and supplement the larger Mexican park would be by creating artificial contours on the United States tract, and emphasizing vertical relief with broad open spaces for public use. The first funds were appropriated in 1968, the site was graded, and irrigation lines and turf were installed to hold down the dust stirred up by spring winds.

One of the first tasks was to discuss the proposed "culture center" with a wide range of local organizations and individuals, to help formulate the plans for development and use. It became clear that the image in the minds of the community leaders was the creation of a medium-sized indoor performing arts facility with an associated visual arts display area. These were included in the plans for the central visitor center, with a small history museum and designs for expansion to add offices, maintenance space and support facilities. The latter proved to be impractical within the funding limitations of P.L. 89-479. Initial funds were appropriated in 1971, and the local firm of Carroll, Daeuble, DuSang and Rand created an award-winning building. The flexible design of the auditorium was by Dr. George Izenour, Professor Emeritus of Theater Architecture at Yale University.

Part of the advance planning also entailed the production of a documentary film, since the broad sweep of the border country could not be readily shown in the limited historical museum planned. The film, *This Most Singular Country*, was given its public premier during the 1972 meeting of the American Association of Museums in Mexico City and received the prestigious Cine Award for cinematography. A second award-winning film, the locally produced *Tapestry*, was filmed largely at Chamizal in 1974 as a tribute to legendary dance teacher Rosa Guerrero.

The Chamizal National Memorial Office in El Paso opened in September 1967 drawing heavily on the United States Section of the IBWC for support and with an especially close relationship to the City Planning Department. Both organizations helped the new Chamizal staff learn about the border community.

Planning for the use of the memorial facilities rested upon the basic concept that the demonstrated friendship of the border could be best served and supported through the display of the arts, formal and informal, graphic and live. Special concessions to local groups were to be combined with imported presentations of the myriad cultural patterns found among the border states. The first event, the Border Folk Festival, was held even before the dedication of the memorial, and on November 17, 1973, the facility was formally opened.

The combination of carefully designed special events and local presentations proved successful. In 1976 the American Revolutionary Bicentennial Commission list of recurring commemorative events for the future included two Chamizal special events, the Border Folk Festival, which then expanded into a larger display of national and international traditional artists, and the new Siglo de Oro Drama Festival, which brought theater companies from Spain together with many nations of the New World in presenting the works of Spain's great theater period of the seventeenth and eighteenth centuries.[10] A later addition was the annual midsummer Festival de la Zarzuela, at which international groups display Spain's lively musical theater form.[11]

With the development of a permanent outdoor stage, in the late 1970s, other events became possible. Since 1985, the Arts Resources

Department of the City of El Paso has presented summer Sunday evening Music Under the Stars concerts to large audiences.

The first major visual arts acquisition was the donation of the Joy and Arthur Addis collection of Twentieth Century Mexican Art in 1979.

Throughout these early years, citizens of El Paso and Ciudad Juárez demonstrated their support with donations of services and gifts to make continued growth possible.

Other actions should be mentioned. On October 21, 1976, Public Law 94-578 increased the authorized development limitation from $2,060,000 to $5,500,000 million. With the cooperation of local charro organizations, a *lienzo de charros*, or performing ring, was added to the memorial, making the sport of *charrería*, the precursor of the North American rodeo, available at the memorial.

Finally, in 1990 the funds for additional facilities at the memorial were appropriated, and in 1991 the new facilities, including improved maintenance and support space, a multi-purpose art display area, offices, and an improved outdoor stage were opened to the public.[12]

Chamizal Memorial remains dedicated to the theme, derived from the long history of the border:

> Men of good will, working together, can reach equitable solutions to mutual problems, and in working together, they will find friendship and gain understanding.

Notes

1. The dates may be confusing: separate actions were required and completed: Convention signed in Mexico City, August 29, 1963; ratification recommended by the United States Senate, December 17, 1963; ratified by President Johnson, December 20, 1963; ratified by Mexico, January 7, 1964; ratification exchanged in Mexico City, January 14, 1964; ratification proclaimed (as of January 14) by President Johnson, January 16, 1964. This confusion has sometimes led to references to the "Chamizal Treaty of 1964.

2. The subtleties of international law and even an understanding of the 1852 boundary and 1864 river channel were rarely developed in the media, and the Chamizal Convention remained a "giveaway" of land in the popular view. This somewhat simplistic view was incorporated into folklore by a popular local musical group:

   "Woke up this mornin', looked out my do'
   Found I was living in old Mexico!
   I got those Chamizal Blues, blue as I can be,
   Cause somebody came and took my house
       away from me!"

   Copyright, 1965, Bob Burns; by
   permission.

3. Unless otherwise noted, all statistical data is drawn from the summary press release of the United States Section, International Boundary and Water Commission 1970, in the Chamizal National Memorial archives.

4. The extent of this is little recognized today, but a friend from graduate school, who had been assigned to the United States Embassy in Santiago, Chile, in the 1950s, told me of an occasion when a United States representative, making the standard statement that the United States had no territorial ambitions south of the Rio Grande, had a heckler shout from the crowd "What about the Chamizal?" (Personal conversation, Dr. James Officer, 1967)

5. Data in this section are taken from the 1964 *Report on the Chamizal Settlement*, Planning Department, City of El Paso.

6. In analyzing these numbers, note that United States Census figures for 1960 show that El Paso had a city population of 276,687—not large in tax base, especially in the perpetually depressed border economy.

7. These four points and the language "national monument and culture center" are constant and consistent in the discussions before the Congress, from the report of the Department of State to the

Senate Foreign Relations Committee on December 12-13, 1963, through the hearings on P.L. 89-479, authorizing the memorial. See especially Senate Report No. 868, 88th Congress, Second Session, February 5, 1964, pages 40 et seq., on Compliance with the Convention on the Chamizal. Unpublished material from various hearings is in the Chamizal files, under Legislative Background.

8. The development of the processes involved in creation of a national park (or other area) is a long and complicated story. The interested reader can find reasonable, objective coverage of the basics in several works:

Ise, John. *Our National Park Policy: A Critical History*. Baltimore, John Hopkins Press, 1961.
Shankland, Robert. *Steve Mather of the National Parks*, 3rd edition. New York, Alfred A. Knopf, 1970.
Swain, Donald C. *Wilderness Defender: Horace M. Albright and Conservation*. Chicago, University of Chicago Press, 1970.

Many other autobiographical works by Conrad Wirth, George Hartzog, and Horace Albright, former directors, and Lemuel Garrison, a major figure in the growth period, are available, and both critics and supporters of the National Park Service have written extensively in recent years.

9. Based on the classification system developed by the National Park Service for the analysis of sites relating to United States history, Chamizal is significant in relation to Great Western Explorations and Political Affairs from 1836 to the present.

10. Outgrowths of the Festival now include presentations of the contracted works in Ciudad Juarez sponsored by the municipality. The University of Texas at El Paso joins with the Association for Classic Hispanic Theater (an academic organization generated by the Festival) in cosponsoring an annual academic symposium. The association also maintains an extensive library of films and videotapes of productions for college ad university use, and sponsors productions of outstanding translations.

11. Without extending the text unduly by including the details of the design and implementation of the "culture center" concept, some aspects and people involved must be included for the historical record. The early input of Edwin Blacker, then assigned to the National Capitol Region of the National Park Service, convinced the Southwest Regional Office and the Washington Office of the

need for a permanent theater technical staff and guided us in the years of 1971-74 toward professional theater operation. The first cultural affairs director of the memorial, E.O. "Skip" Larsen, implemented the programming and established a tradition of excellence. His successor, Walker M. Reid (1974-93) expanded the programming and was instrumental in the establishment and growth of the Siglo de Oro Drama Festival and the Zarzuela Festival. Carlos Chavez, of Reid's staff, managed the Border Folk Festival for eighteen years and first saw the opportunity of including charrería in the cultural presentations. More than sixty other Chamizal staff members contributed, very frequently far beyond duty hours or job requirements. Paseños ranged from city officials to staff members of the Festival Association for the Performing Arts, who provided productions of superb quality for three years, 1973-75, and the El Paso Arts Council, whose film series was especially welcome.

The most important National Park Service figure was Frank F. Kowski, Regional Director, Southwest Region, with the very supportive staff he led during the planning and first years of operation, notably regional historian William E. Brown. It was Kowski's personal conviction and impressive support which led to the final decision to include a performing arts capability in the initial development in 1973.

12. A mural, "Nuestra Herencia" (Our Heritage) specifically designed for the border by El Paso artist Carlos Flores, was added to the wall facing Mexico in 1993 as a result of a donation from the Junior League of El Paso.

Index